Writing
Strands

A COMPLETE WRITING PROGRAM
USING A PROCESS APPROACH
TO WRITING AND COMPOSITION

ASSURING
CONTINUITY AND CONTROL

LEVEL 4

of
a complete writing program
for homeschoolers

a
publication
of

NATIONAL WRITING INSTITUTE
624 W. University #248
Denton, TX 76201-1889

Manufactured in the United States of America

ISBN 978-1-888344-09-7

For information: National Writing Institute,
                      624 W. University #248
                      Denton, TX 76201-1889

                      (800) 688-5375
                      info@writingstrands.com

Cover art by Matt Payovich

NATIONAL WRITING INSTITUTE PUBLICATIONS

STUDENTS

Writing Strands Level 1
Writing Strands Level 2
Writing Strands Level 3
Writing Strands Level 4
Writing Strands Level 5
Writing Strands Level 6
Writing Strands Level 7
Writing Exposition
Creating Fiction

Communication And Interpersonal Relationships

Dragonslaying Is For Dreamers
Axel Meets The Blue Men
Axel's Challenge

PARENTS/TEACHERS

Evaluating Writing

Reading Strands

Analyzing The Novel:
Dragonslaying Is For Dreamers

Essays on Writing

INTRODUCTION

This group of exercises in the series called *Writing Strands* is designed to give homeschooled students a grounding in the very complicated process of giving others their thoughts in written form. This level is designed for any student who has completed the exercises in *Writing Strands* 3 or students who, in public school, would be considered ready for eighth or ninth grade. Of course, forth and ninth grade students would write much differently, but that is not a problem. Both levels of students can benefit from learning the skills presented in this level. It has been designed to be widely applied, and there are many experiences here that most young writers should have.

Learning to write skillfully is one of the hardest jobs that you have. These exercises will make it easier. Much of the planning and detail of the writing process is presented here.

The writing exercises in this level are in four categories: basic, creation, organization, and description. The exercises in each of these areas will guide you in the development of the skills you'll need.

Rather than increase the work for your parents, this writing process should make it easier for both you and your parents to meet the demands for student writing skill.

When these exercises are completed, you will have a well-founded introduction to this most difficult skill, and your parents will find it easier to have confidence that this part of the teaching challenge has been met.

For most students there are about 90 days of writing instruction in this book. When you finish each writing exercise, if you then spend about a week reading and discussing ideas with your parents, you will have a language arts program that will last you for a full year. If you are an older student doing some catch up, that's fine, finish sooner.

CONTENTS

HOW TO MAKE *WRITING STRANDS* WORK FOR YOU

1. You should have a writing folder containing all of your written work which should be kept for your next level. This will give you a place to store and record your skills, and it's a great thing for your parents to have if they have to make a report on your progress.

2. You and your parents should track what you have learned and what you still need to learn. Here are some ways to do that:
   a) After every assignment, you should fill in the record of progress which follows the assignment.
   b) Your parents should fill out the Writing Skills Mastery as you complete assignments.
   c) Writers can always learn new things and young writers shouldn't expect to fix all their problems right away. Your parents can keep track of the problems they've noted but you haven't yet solved using using the "Spelling List" and "List of Problems to Solve".

3. Each exercise begins with a suggested time for completion. Of course, all students work at different rates. The suggested daily activities can be combined or extended depending on your desire and your goals.

4. Many of the exercises suggest that your parents will work with you during your writing period reading what you have written. If this is done, it will serve two purposes:
   a) It will give you constant feedback and will allow your parents to catch many writing problems before they appear in your final papers.
   b) It will greatly cut down on your parents' correcting time. Most of the proofreading can be done during your writing time, so, even though you will be writing much more than you previously have been, your parents should be able to help you more using even less time.

5. Your parents should use the book *Evaluating Writing* to help them and you with your writing. If they do, it will help you both a great deal with the development of your skills.

6. It might be good if you don't write in this book at all but use other paper and make copies of those pages at the end of each semester's work where you can list the problems you've solved and the ones at the end of each exercise called "Record of Progress." This way your book will be completely clean for your younger brothers or sisters to use.

PRINCIPLES

The following principles were adopted by National Writing Institute before work began on *Writing Strands*. They were our guides in the initial stages of the design of the exercises.

1. Every person needs to learn to express ideas and feelings in writing.

2. There is no one right way to write anything.

3. The ability to write is not an expression of a body of knowledge that can be learned like a list of vocabulary words.

4. Writing teachers and their students both learn in any effective writing situation.

5. The product of each student's writing efforts must be seen as a success for at least the following reasons:
   a) A student in a writing situation is not in competition with anyone else.
   b) There is no perfect model against which any effort can be compared for evaluation, so there is no best way for any student to write.
   c) Every controlled writing experience will help students improve the ability to express themselves.

6. All student writing efforts are worthy of praise. The most help any writing teacher can give at any point is to show, in a positive way, what is good about a piece and how it might be improved.

7. Any writing lesson assigned which is done independently by the student and does not have a teacher's constant feedback in the form of reinforcement and suggestions represents a missed opportunity for the student.

8. All writing at any level is hard work and every writer should be encouraged to feel the pride of authorship.

9. All young authors need to be published. This can be accomplished by having their work read to other family members, posted on bulletin boards (refrigerators), printed in "books" or read by other family members.

10. Students should learn that writing is fun, exciting and rewarding. This cannot be taught to a student who is punished by being made to write. Punishments, such as writing fifty times "I will not argue with my brothers" will certainly destroy the joy of learning to write.

EXERCISES * SKILLS AREAS * OBJECTIVES

Exercise 1: **How a Sentence Does It**
Skill Area : Basic

Objectives: 1. Decide what information you want to give to your reader
              2. Organize this information for your reader
              3. Write a sentence containing the information in that order

Exercise 2: **Connections**
Skill Area: Organization

Objectives: 1. Understanding that ideas in sentences are connected
             2. Understanding that ideas flow from one sentence to the next
             3. Writing with ideas flowing from one point to another

Exercise 3: **The Main Points**
Skill Area: Organization

Objectives: 1. Recognizing the main points in a story
             2. Listing the main points in the summary of a story

Exercise 4: **I Feel**
Skill Area: Creative

Objectives: 1. Recognizing emotional reactions
             2. Deciding how to describe reactions
             3. Describing emotions

Exercise 5: **My Mistake**
Skill Area: Organization

             1. Thinking through actions
             2. Analyzing actions
             3. Recognizing what actions may lead to

Exercise 6: **What the Narrative Voice Tells the Reader**
Skill Area: Creative

Objectives: 1. Understanding that there is a voice which speaks to the reader
2. Understanding that a choice of voices must be made
3. Choosing a voice to tell a story

Exercise 7: **Changing Tenses**
Skill Area: Basic

Objectives: 1. Understanding past tense
2. Understanding how changing tenses changes the narration
3. Changing past tense to present tense

Exercise 8: **Paragraphs**
Skill Area: Basic

Objectives: 1. Organizing a group of ideas
2. Writing a sentence that introduces a list of ideas
3. Constructing a paragraph

Exercise 9: **My Home (1)**
Skill Area: Description

Objectives: 1. Understanding the layout of a building
2. Showing size relationships of spaces
3. Using a bird's-eye view
4. Changing visual into graphic form

Exercise 10: **My Home (2)**
Skill Area: Description

Objectives: 1. Understanding the structure of description
2. Starting descriptions with general statements
3. Supporting with detail
4. Turning graphic representations into verbal descriptions

Exercise 11: **My Home (3)**
Skill Area: Description

Objectives: 1. Writing an accurate description
           2. Evaluating own work
           3. Rewriting to improve work

Exercise 12: **Describing a Thought Problem**
Skill Area: Organization

Objective: 1. Picturing a situation
           2. Describing a situation
           3. Understanding how people would act in a problem situation
           4. Solving a thought problem

Exercise 13: **Person**
Skill Area: Basic

Objectives: 1. Using first person
           2. Using third person
           3. Avoiding careless use of second person
           4. Controlling use of person in writing

Exercise 14: **Past, Present and Future**
Skill Area: Basic

Objectives: 1. Using past tense
           2. Using present tense
           3. Using future tense

Exercise 15: **Things Change**
Skill Area: Description

Objectives: 1. Understanding that objects change
           2. Organizing observations
           3. Describing changes in an organized way

Exercise 16: **From Where I Was**
Skill Area: Creative

Objectives: 1. Understanding character positions
           2. Realizing how position controls what characters understand
           3. Placing characters in positions in first person narration

Exercise 17: **Attitude in Description**
Skill Area: Description

Objectives: 1. Understanding that authors give attitudes to their
             narrative voices
           2. Giving readers feelings by the methods of description used

Exercise 18: **The Long and Short of It**
Skill Area: Creative

Objectives: 1. Understanding that sentence length is important
           2. Realizing that sentence length control helps readers
             understand what a writer is saying
           3. Controlling sentence lengths for reader understanding

STRANDS

This writing program has been designed to start with very simple directions to produce very simple writing. You'll find that the work will get harder as you progress. This is not all bad. You should expect to get better at writing as you practice.

To help you and your parents understand how this progression of difficulty works, I have listed below, the strands, the exercises that present the strands and where they are found in this text. Do the assignments in the sequence they are presented in, not in the order below.

NOT RULES, MORE LIKE SUGGESTIONS

In almost everything we do, there are rules (like laws), and then there are what we call "rules." The rules that are like laws are written and we all accept these as the rules we have to live by. Then there are the "rules," the things that we *should* do, that we agree to do, and things that make life nicer for everyone if we do them.

This is also true in writing. As an example of the difference in the rules of writing, look at the rule (law) that says that every sentence must start with a capital letter. This is written down and we all must write using this rule. A "rule" of writing is that we use an exclamation point only once a year.

The following "rules" are just strong suggestions. You can violate them if you want to. It might be good to keep in mind however, that if you do, your readers will look at your writing the same way that the company at dinner might look at you if you burped at the end of the meal. So, below is a short list of the "rules" of writing:

1. Don't use exclamation points! This makes any writing look amateurish and fuzzy. If you're saying something that's important, the way you say it should be strong enough so that you don't have to tell your reader that it's important by using exclamation points at the end of your sentences.

2. Don't underline the titles of your papers. The only time there should be an underline in one of your titles is when you use the names of books or magazines.

3. Skip a line after the title in any paper you're giving to someone else to read.

4. Never write *The End* at the end of anything you write for a schooling exercise.

5. Don't try writing humor until you've studied it and really know the difference between being funny and being corny. (Those places in this book where I've tried to be funny and was corny will give you an example of what I mean.)

6. Don't skip a line between paragraphs.

7. Always leave a margin at the bottom of each page.

8. Check your papers for clichés before you write the final drafts.

WRITING SKILLS MASTERY

WRITING STRANDS 4 EXERCISES

Parents: Below is a list of each assignment's objectives. As your student completes an assignment, indicate whether each objective has been met. If your child needs experience with an objective, revisit this assignment or this skill before proceeding to the next *Writing Strands* level.

Student Name:_____ Date:_____

Skill   Needs
Mastered   Experience

Exercise 1: How a Sentence Does it
Skill Area: Basic

_____   _____ 1. Writing with ideas flowing from one point to another
_____   _____ 2. Organizing this information for your reader
_____   _____ 3. Writing a sentence containing the information in that order

Exercise 2: Connections
Skill Area: Organization

_____   _____ 1. Understanding that ideas in sentences are connected
_____   _____ 2. Understanding that ideas flow from one sentence to the next
_____   _____ 3. Writing with ideas flowing from one sentence to another

Exercise 3: The Main Points
Skill Area: Organization

_____   _____ 1. Recognizing the main points in a story
_____   _____ 2. Listing the main points in the summary of a story

Exercise 4: I Feel
Skill Area: Creative

_____   _____ 1. Recognizing emotional reactions
_____   _____ 2. Deciding how to describe reactions
_____   _____ 3. Describing emotions

Skill   Needs
Mastered   Experience

Exercise 5: My Mistake
Skill Area: Organization
_____   _____ 1. Thinking through actions
_____   _____ 2. Analyzing actions
_____   _____ 3. Recognizing what actions lead to mistakes

Exercise 6: What the Narrative Voice Tells the Reader
Skill Area: Creative
_____   _____ 1. Understanding that there's a voice which speaks to the reader
_____   _____ 2. Understanding that there can be different voices
_____   _____ 3. Choosing a voice to tell a story

Exercise 7: Point of View
Skill Area: Basic
_____   _____ 1. Understanding past tense
_____   _____ 2. Understanding how changing tenses changes a narration
_____   _____ 3. Changing past tense to present tense

Exercise 8: Paragraphs
Skill Area: Basic
_____   _____ 1. Organizing a group of ideas
_____   _____ 2. Writing a sentence that introduces a list of ideas
_____   _____ 3. Constructing a paragraph

Exercise 9: My Home (1)
Skill Area: Description
_____   _____ 1. Understanding the layout of a building
_____   _____ 2. Showing size relationships of spaces
_____   _____ 3. Using a bird's-eye view
_____   _____ 4. Changing visual images into graphic form

Skill   Needs
Mastered   Experience

Exercise 10: My Home (2)
Skill Area: Description
____   ____ 1. Understanding the structure of description
____   ____ 2. Starting descriptions with general statements
____   ____ 3. Supporting with detail
____   ____ 4. Turning graphic representations into verbal descriptions

Exercise 11: My Home (3)
Skill Area: Description
____   ____ 1. Writing an accurate description
____   ____ 2. Evaluating own work
____   ____ 3. Rewriting to improve work

Exercise 12: Describing a Thought Problem
Skill Area: Organization

____   ____ 1. Picturing a situation
____   ____ 2. Describing a situation
____   ____ 3. Understanding how people would act in a problem situation
____   ____ 4. Solving a thought problem

Exercise 13: Person
Skill Area: Basic

____   ____ 1. Using first person
____   ____ 2. Using third person
____   ____ 3. Avoiding careless use of second person
____   ____ 4. Controlling use of person in writing

Exercise 14: Past, Present and Future
Skill Area: Basic

____   ____ 1. Using past tense
____   ____ 2. Using present tense
____   ____ 3. Using future tense

Skill   Needs
Mastered   Experience

Exercise 15: Things Change
Skill Area: Descriptive

_____   _____ 1. Understanding that objects change
_____   _____ 2. Organizing observations
_____   _____ 3. Describing changes in an organized way

Exercise 16: From Where I Was
Skill Area: Creative

_____   _____ 1. Understanding character positions
_____   _____ 2. Realizing how position controls what characters understand
_____   _____ 3. Placing characters in positions in first person narration

Exercise 17: Attitude in Description
Skill Area: Descriptive

_____   _____ 1. Understanding that authors give attitudes to their narrative voices
_____   _____ 2. Giving readers feelings by the methods of description used

Exercise 18: The Long and Short of It
Skill Area: Creative

_____   _____ 1. Understanding that sentence length is important
_____   _____ 2. Realizing that sentence length control helps readers understand what a
                        writer is saying
_____   _____ 3. Controlling sentence lengths for reader understanding

SPELLING LIST

The research on how people learn to spell indicates that spelling mastery comes from using words. Words studied in isolation, in abstracted lists, do not carry over from the study to correct use.

This page is not to be used as a word list to be memorized. Rather it is for you to keep a record of the words your children have problems with. Turn back to this page after each exercise and record the words that you want each child to work on in the future weeks.

If you were to pick out one word a week—one that your children uses constantly—and you were to work that week with that one problem word, in two or three years your children would have mastered hundreds of words, and not have experienced the frustration of testing and failure.

You could use a large dictionary to find the derivation, study the prefixes and suffixes and the basic spelling rules that apply. If you were to make sure that that word were used correctly in all of the work that week, and from then on, you would see that spelling would improve much more than it has by studying lists of words.

You might check our book *Evaluating Writing* for more on this subject.

_____·_____

_____·_____

_____·_____

_____·_____

_____·_____

_____·_____

_____·_____

_____·_____

_____·_____

_____·_____

LIST OF PROBLEMS TO SOLVE

Student Name:_____Date:_____

    As you and your child work through this book, use this page as a convenient place to keep a running list of the problems you feel should be solved throughout the year.

    Keep in mind that you will have years to work with each child, and you won't be able to make any of them perfect this week or month or even this year. Record here the writing problems (for whatever reason) your child has not yet solved. If you point out to each child only one way to improve in mechanics each exercise, that would be fine. In a very few years you would have helped each child much more than you would if you were to point out everything that was wrong with each writing. Check our book *Evaluating Writing* for more on this process and why it is so very important for you and your children.

_____._____

_____._____

_____._____

_____._____

_____._____

_____._____

_____._____

_____._____

_____._____

_____._____

#4 I FEEL

SKILL: DESCRIPTION

It may take you four days to:
1. Decide how you felt about something that happened to you
2. Understand that it is possible to explain how you felt about an event
3. Describe how you felt about an event

PREWRITING

Days One and Two:

It's hard for some people to talk about how they feel, but this exercise will make it easy for you to write about how you felt about something that happened to you.

There are lots of different ways to feel about some other person, a place you've been or something that's happened to you.

In fact, everything you have ever done has made you feel some way. Every time you go into your house you feel something. When you sit down to dinner you feel. When you walk into a library you have feelings. When you see the check-out lady at the grocery store you feel something about her or about your parents paying for the food.

If you follow the steps below, you'll be able to describe how you felt about something so other people, who read what you've written, will understand how and why you felt that way.

WRITING:

There are 4 steps used in describing how you felt about something.

Step 1. You'll have to pick an event you've been involved in. It doesn't have to be an important thing at all. Anything will do.

Step 2. Decide how you felt about this event. Try and write this in one word.

Step 3. List the things you saw, heard and touched that made you feel that way.

Step 4. Put all of this together in an explanation of how you felt.

I'll list these four points to show you how easy this is: (Check the above list as you read this example for how each of the four points works.)

Step 1. (Event) *I had to walk to the car in the rain today.*

Step 2. (How I felt) *First mad, then glad.*

Step 3. (What I saw, heard and touched) *I saw, heard and touched things that changed how I felt.*

    A) I saw water on the car.
    B) I saw rain falling.
    C) I heard rain on the roof of the car.
    D) I saw puddles of water in the driveway.
    E) I felt rain on my face and hands.
    F) I could smell the rain.

Step 4. (Put all this together)

At first I was mad when I walked to the car in the rain today but that changed. I knew it was raining when I saw water standing on the finish of the car. The drops hit the metal top with a ping. There were puddles of water standing in the driveway. When I stepped off the porch, I could feel the rain on my face and hands. I could even smell it. It smelled like spring. This made me glad that winter was about over and that spring would soon be here, and when I thought of that, I was no longer mad but was glad that it was raining.

I'll take apart this paragraph and label where the pieces of it came from.

(Topic Sentence) *At first I was mad when I walked to the car in the rain today but that changed.*

(Saw) *I knew it was raining when I saw water standing on the finish of the car.*

(Heard) *The drops hit the metal top with a ping.*

(Saw) *There were puddles of water standing in the driveway.*

(Felt) *When I stepped off the porch, I could feel the rain on my face and hands.*

(Smelled) *I could even smell it. It smelled like spring.*

(How this changed how
I felt about the rain) *This made me glad that winter was about over and that spring would soon be here, and when I thought of that, I was no longer mad but was glad that it was raining.*

Day Three:

You're to do this exercise just the same way that I did. On other paper use the list of 4 points.

Step 1. (Event)_____

Step 2. (How you felt)_____

Step 3. (List of experiences. Check my list to see how to make your list.)

        A)_____

        B)_____

        C)_____

        D)_____

        E)_____

Step 4. (On other paper write the description of how you felt)

_____

_____

_____

_____

_____

_____

> **Hint: A compound sentence is two complete sentences joined by a comma and a conjunction (and, but, or). Try one.**

Day Four:

You now have the **body** of a paragraph. You need a **topic sentence** and then you'll have a complete paragraph.

A topic sentence tells the reader what kinds of information will be in the paragraph. You'll have to think of a sentence that will tell your reader that you had feelings about something that happened to you. (*Good spot for a compound sentence.*)

This topic sentence will be the first sentence in your paragraph. It could say something simple like: *I felt good today*, or *I was embarrassed yesterday*, or *I was glad it was Saturday.* Write your topic sentence for your paragraph on other paper.

_____

_____

On other paper put the pieces of your paragraph together.

Set your paper up this way: Your **name** and **date** in the upper right corner. **Skip two spaces**. Write a **title** for your paper on the first line of the page. Make it simple like, *I Feel.* **Skip one line** and write your **paragraph** starting with your **topic sentence**. Check this example paper outline.

```
                                                      (Your Name)
                                                      (The Date)
    (Skip two spaces)
                              (Your Title)
    (Skip one line)
                            (Your paragraph)
    (Indent topic sentence)



    (Make equal margins for all edges of page)

              (Page numbers bottom center)
```

| **Hint: A semicolon can be used to join two complete sentences.** |

Fill out the "Record of Progress" on the next page. I recommend you now take a week off from writing and concentrate on reading and discussing ideas with your parents.

RECORD OF PROGRESS

Name: _____ Date: _____

Exercise **#4 I FEEL**
This is the best sentence I wrote this week.

_____

_____

This mistake I made this week and I will not make it next week.

_____

_____

This is the sentence that had this mistake in it.

_____

_____

This is the sentence again showing how I fixed this mistake.

_____

_____

Comments:

#5 MY MISTAKE

SKILL: ORGANIZATION

It may take you three days to learn to:
1. Admit that you did something that was a mistake
2. Analyze what you did
3. Recognize the action that caused the mistake

PREWRITING

Day One:

We all make mistakez. (⊃ee?) This isn't a bad thing to do. It's how we learn. If we didn't make mistakes, we wouldn't learn.

Here are the steps you'll use to write this paper:

1. **Name a mistake** you've made.
2. **List the actions** that led to the mistake.
3. **Decide** which actions caused the mistake.
4. Figure out what you **could have done** to avoid the mistake.
5. **Describe the changes** you'll make in your actions so you won't make that same mistake again.

I did this exercise for a mistake I made. I numbered the above points in the paragraph so you could see how they fit. I labeled the topic sentence **(TS)**.

   (TS) ___Last night I made a mistake as I was helping my wife do the dishes.___ *I carried the dishes from the table to the counter. When I piled the dinner plates on the counter,* **(2)** ___I didn't take the silverware off the plates___ *first. This made the plates wobbly.* **(1)** *When I put the* ___fourth plate on the stack___ *on the counter and turned back for another load, the top* ___plate slipped___ *off the pile and broke on the floor.* **(3)** *It was* ___leaving the knifes and forks on the plates that___ *caused them to tip off the counter.* **(4)** *They* ___should have been taken off each plate___ *as it was stacked.* **(5)** *If my wife lets me help her do the dishes again,* ___I'll put the silverware to one side when I stack the plates.___

Day Two:

Here is the list of steps I developed when I analyzed my mistake:

1. I carried piles of dirty dishes from the table to the counter.
2. I didn't take the silverware off the plates before I piled them on the counter.
3. I put another plate on top of the pile of plates that still had silverware on them.

Make a short list on other paper of mistakes you've made sometime in the past.

1. _____

2. _____

3. _____

Ask your parent to look at this list and help you pick out a mistake that would be easy for you to analyze. Make a list, like below, of the actions that you took in making that mistake. This list doesn't need to be in sentences. Use words or phrases if you want to.

1. Carried pile of dishes to counter
2. Didn't remove silverware
3. Piled plates on each other with silverware on them

List the actions that led to your mistake on a separate sheet similar to the listing above. These don't have to be full sentences.

1. _____

2. _____

3. _____

Day Three:

Turn yesterday's list of actions into complete sentences.

1. _____

   _____

2. _____

   _____

3. _____

_____

Write a topic sentence that tells your reader what your paragraph is about. It can be like mine when I wrote that I made a mistake when I was helping my wife. (Try a compound sentence using just a semicolon.)

_____

_____

Below is a chart showing what this paper should look like when you're finished.

(Your Name)
(Date)
(Skip two spaces)
Exercise #5: My Mistake
(Skip one line)
(List of Actions Causing Mistake)
1.   3.
2.   4.
(Action List Turned Into Sentences)
1.
2.
3.
4.
(Topic sentence for the paragraph):
(Indent your topic sentence)
(Page numbers bottom center & even margins all around)

Fill out the "Record of Progress" on the next page. I recommend you now take a week off from writing and concentrate on reading and discussing ideas with your parents.

RECORD OF PROGRESS

Name: _____ Date: _____

Exercise **#5 MY MISTAKE**

This is the best sentence I wrote this week.

_____

_____

This mistake I made this week and I will not make it next week.

_____

_____

This is the sentence that had this mistake in it.

_____

_____

This is the sentence again showing how I fixed this mistake.

_____

_____

Comments:

#6 WHAT THE NARRATIVE VOICE TELLS THE READER

SKILL: CREATION

It may take you six days to learn that:
1. Writers create voices which speak to their readers
2. All the voices writers use do not work the same way
3. When you write, you too, must choose a voice to talk to your reader

PREWRITING

Day One:

If we worked together with the book, *Writing Strands Level 3*, you've been introduced to the idea of the "voice" of a storyteller. If you didn't use that book, this idea may be new to you. If it is, that's good, too.

Writers must talk to their readers because that's what writing is all about. But, a writer can't speak directly to any reader. This voice must come from the pages of writing. This voice writers create is called the **narrative voice.**

This created voice tells the story. The writer writes the words on the page, but the real teller of the story is the **narrative voice** who says the words to the reader. If this isn't clear, ask your parent to discuss this idea with you.

This narrative voice can even be **a character** in the story. (Ask your parent to talk about this idea. It can get complicated, and it's very important that you understand it.)

When the narrative voice is a character in the story, it means that the **voice is a person in the story**, and the voice speaks in **first person** and sounds like this:

> *I saw the dog that had been lost by the rich man, and I wanted to make sure he got his dog back and that I got the reward.*

The *I* in this example is **both the narrative voice and a character in the story**. If this isn't clear to you, ask your parent for help. You must understand this idea.

When the **narrative voice is not a character** in the story but is what is called a **non-character**, then the **voice is not part of the story**. This voice sounds like it's standing outside of the story looking in and, speaking in **third person**, tells the reader what happens to the people in the story. This **non-character voice** sounds like this:

<u>**The young boy**</u> *saw the lost dog, and* <u>**the boy**</u> *wanted the rich man to get his dog back and to be sure* <u>**he**</u> *got the reward.*

The main difference in these two voices is that:

1. **The first narrative voice**, which **is a character** in the story, speaks in **first person** and uses the word, **I**.

2. **The second narrative voice**, which **is not a character** in the story, speaks in **third person** and uses the words, *she, he* or *they*.

What I want you to understand is that there are **two main narrative voices**.

Narrative voice #1. The **narrative voice who is a character** in the story, who speaks in **first person** and tells the reader what happens.

Narrative voice #2. The **narrative voice who is outside the story** and watches characters in the story and speaks in **third person** and tells the reader what happens.

A writer must be careful not to mix up these two narrative voices in one story.

Day Two:

When a **narrative voice is a character** in a story and this voice speaks in **first person**, using the word, *I,* the narrative voice cannot know what other characters are thinking. This is because characters are not mind readers. (Ask *your parent about this idea.*)

This narrative voice can tell the reader what he or she (the narrative voice) is thinking, but that's all this character/voice can tell about what's going on in anyone's mind.

You'll start a very short story about a dog and its trainer. You'll have to tell your reader what the dog's thinking. You'll not be able to tell your reader what the man's thinking because you'll be using the first person voice to tell the story. (This *character/narrative voice will be the voice of the dog.*)

I'll start the story for you. Your job will be to finish the story using **first person** and the **limited knowledge** which a character would have. **Limited knowledge** means that the <u>**voice cannot get into the minds of the other characters.**</u> I have made bold the use of **first person** in the very short example below. This **narrative voice** has **no way of knowing** what's in the man's mind.

> *When the man brought **me** home from the pound, **I** realized there was a lot he had to learn. He knew almost nothing about how to treat dogs.*
> *At first **I** thought that it would be easy to train him, but, after the second day, **I** knew **I** had a real job on **my** paws. One of the first things **I** had to teach him was when to let **me** out. He was a very slow learner. **I** didn't want to do it, but sometimes **I** even had to scratch on the door to get him to act right.*
> *Another problem **I** had was teaching him about fresh water. . .*

You'll notice that the dog's voice is the voice the writer has created to talk to the reader. This dog/narrative voice is using **first person** and the word, *I*.

WRITING

Days Three and Four:
You're to finish this very short story about training the dog owner.

You **must stay in first person,** and the **narrative voice** must remain **limited** to what **the dog/character/narrative voice** could know.

Days Five and Six:
Rewrite the same story, but now it'll be told to the reader by a narrative voice which is **not** part of the story—**not a character**. In this example, I have made bold the use of **third person**—the narrative voice (not a character in the story), using the word, *he, she* or *they*.

Notice that this voice **can get into the minds of both the man and the dog** and tell the reader what they **both are thinking**. (This narrative voice is called omniscient)

> *The day **the man** brought **the dog** home from the pound it looked like **they** would get along fine. But later that evening the trouble started. **The dog** began to scratch on the door. **The man** thought to himself, "He just came in. He can't have to go out already." **The man** figured that if **he** just ignored the dog, **it** would forget about going out. **He** didn't know that's not how it is with dogs.*
> ***The dog thought** that the man would never learn to deal with **a dog** the way he should.*

You're to finish this short story using **third person** and an **omniscient narrative voice. Omniscient** means that the narrative voice **tells the reader** what the two characters (the man and the dog) are thinking. Set your paper up to be like the example on the next page.

```
┌─────────────────────────────────────────────────────────────────────┐
│                                                   (Your Name)         │
│                                                   (The date)          │
│ (Skip two spaces)                                                     │
│                                                                       │
│            (The Title):  #6 What the Narrative Voice Tells the Reader │
│ (Skip one line)                                                       │
│                       (First person, limited voice)                   │
│                                                                       │
│                    (Third person, limited omniscient voice)           │
│                                                                       │
│                                                                       │
│                  (Remember the margins and page numbers)              │
│                                                                       │
└─────────────────────────────────────────────────────────────────────┘
```

When you're done with this exercise, you could define the following terms for your parent to demonstrate that you're learning good stuff. First, talk to your parent about the differences in the narrative voices in each story. Then read your two stories out loud.

Be sure and use the words below when you talk about the differences in the two narrative voices. Cover the following five points. You might start by describing what a narrative voice does.

1. Narrative voice: (What is a narrative voice and what are the two kinds used in the two
            stories?)
2. First person: (What does 1st person sound like and what can't it talk about?)
3. Third person: (What does 3rd person sound like and what can it talk about?)
4. Omniscient: (What does this word mean and what does it allow the third person narrative
            voice to talk about?)
5. Limited Omniscient: (What's the difference because the word, limited, has been added?)

┌───┐
│ **Hint: A dash says: explanation follows.**   │
│ **A colon says: information follows.**   │
└───┘

Fill out the "Record of Progress" on the next page. I recommend you now take a week off from writing and concentrate on reading and discussing ideas with your parents.

RECORD OF PROGRESS

Name: _____ Date: _____

Exercise **#6 WHAT THE NARRATIVE VOICE TELLS THE READER**

This is the best sentence I wrote this week.

_____

_____

This mistake I made this week and I will not make it next week.

_____

_____

This is the sentence that had this mistake in it.

_____

_____

This is the sentence again showing how I fixed this mistake.

_____

_____

Comments:

#7 CHANGING TENSES

SKILL: BASIC

It may take you three days to learn to:
1. Understand how past tense works
2. Understand how a change from past to present tense in a story changes the story.
3. Change past tense to present tense in a story

PREWRITING

Days One and Two:

Most stories are written in past tense, but there are a very few that are written in present tense. In this exercise you'll have a chance to change the tense of a story from **past tense to present tense.**

Past tense talks about things that have already happened.   Bill **saw** the dog.

Present tense talks about things that are happening at the time of the reading. Bill **sees** the dog. Or Bill **is seeing** the dog.

The following examples will show you how this is done.

PAST TENSE: *When Mary **put** her shoes on after swimming, she **felt** the frog that Bill **had put there** when nobody **was** looking.*

PRESENT TENSE: *When Mary **puts** her shoes on after swimming, she **feels** the frog Bill **has put there** when nobody was looking*

You're to work with any story or book of fiction that your parent agrees for you to use. This narrative should be written in **past tense**. The first words on the first page and first line on the next page and the first few lines on the last page will tell you if this writer is consistent in the use of tenses.

> **Hint: Your narrative voice tense should be consistent.**

WRITING

Turn part of this story into present tense. It'll be like you and the writer are working together on the story. You'll have to pick two pages of the story and **change the tense to present tense**. It'll be like you're rewriting that part of the story. You should set your paper up following the directions below:

1. **Your name** (first, last and the date) should be in the upper right hand corner.
2. There should be a **title on the first line**. No quote marks or underlining and there should be capitals.
3. **Skip** the second line and **start** your paper about your two-page rewriting on the **third line** of the paper.
4. You should start by **identifying the pages** (by number) you have rewritten.
5. Give the **name of the story.**
6. Identify who has rewritten the two pages of it. (*your name*)
7. Skip a line and start the rewriting.

Julie Wiggins
December 2, 2001

(Skip two spaces)

#7 Changing Tenses

(Skip one line)
Pages_____and_____of__ (Name of the story) _____ rewritten by

(Your name)_____

(Your two pages of the story rewritten)

(Page numbers at bottom center)

Day Three:

The two pages you give to your parent of the story rewritten in present tense should not be from your little sister's picture book. It would be a good experience for you to read what you've written to someone else before you give it to your parent. You might start the story a page or two before the place where you have rewritten it, and, when you're done reading, you might ask your listener what there was about the story that was strange or out of place. This is to see if the shifting of tenses is noticed by your listener.

Fill out the "Record of Progress" on the next page. I recommend you now take a week off from writing and concentrate on reading and discussing ideas with your parents.

RECORD OF PROGRESS

Name: _____ Date: _____

Exercise **#7 CHANGING TENSES**

This is the best sentence I wrote this week.

_____

_____

This mistake I made this week and I will not make it next week.

_____

_____

This is the sentence that had this mistake in it.

_____

_____

This is the sentence again showing how I fixed this mistake.

_____

_____

Comments:

#8 PARAGRAPHS

SKILL: BASIC

It should take you three days to learn how to:
1. Organize a group of ideas
2. Write a sentence that introduces a group of ideas
3. Construct a paragraph based on a group of ideas

PREWRITING

Day One:

There's much more to being an adult than just growing older. Thinking clearly and presenting ideas well to others is another way of being grown up. The more experience people have with using their language, the better they get at it. It would be a shame if people didn't get any better at using their language as they got older.

An important way to learn to use language effectively is to write it. It takes practice to be good at anything, and it'll take practice using your language to be able to use it as well as your parents do or as well as your older friends do.

One difference between the way children use language and the way adults use it, is that many adults organize what they say. This is especially true when they write. It's an important skill to be able to write organized and well-put-together information.

A good place to start is with a paragraph. There are six steps to writing an organized paragraph. This exercise will give you practice in all six.

STEP ONE: Break the subject into parts.

Any subject you want to write a paragraph about you must be able to break into parts. You just have to decide what the parts are.

Let's pretend we've been assigned to write a paper about a child's doll. Upon breaking the idea of a doll into its parts, we'd find that it has different kinds of parts. Some of them would be physical parts, and some of them would be non-physical.

36

First, let's look at the physical parts of a doll. There are:

1. Two arms
   A. Two elbows
   B. Two hands
2. Two legs
   A. Two knees
   B. Two feet
3. One head
   A. Two eyes
   B. One nose
   C. One mouth
   D. Hair
   E. Two ears
4. One body
   A. Chest
   B. Torso
   C. Hips—and so on

Now look at the non-physical parts of a doll. The idea of dolls can be broken into their:

1. Types
   A. Barbie doll
   B. Baby doll
   C. Display doll (The kind adults collect and display on shelves.)
   D. Paper doll
   E. Cabbage Patch
   F. Raggedy -Ann
2. Function
   A. Dependent (baby needs a mother)
   B. Independent (GI Joe type)

We now have a list of the parts of a doll. The list could be physical parts or non-physical parts. We really have enough parts here for lots of paragraphs. We could use just the first list to make our paragraph. This list has four parts:

1. Arms   2. Legs   3. Head   4. Body

Using this list, our paragraph would have at least four sentences in it.

> **Hint: When you organize your material, organize your reader's mind.**

Day Two:

    STEP TWO: Organize the list.

We have to decide in what order we want the sentences. There are a number of ways to order (organize) the items in a paragraph. Some of these ways are:

1. By **size**
2. By **beauty**—the most beautiful first, the second most beautiful next and so on
3. By **importance**
4. By **cost**
5. By **time**—what happened first, what happened next and so on
6. By what you **like** most first, and what you like second next and so on
7. By **top to bottom** or **right to left**

Let's use number seven, top to bottom. That makes sense when talking about a doll. The order of the parts of our paragraph about the doll is:

1. Head
2. Body
3. Arms
4. Legs

This will give us the order and the structure of our paragraph. Let's start with point number one, the head. We have to decide if we can tell our readers all they need to know about our doll's head in just a few sentences. Look at the items under head—there are five things we would have to talk about. We might have to use five sentences just about the head.

STEP THREE: Narrow the topic. (Write about just a small part of the original topic.)

Let's not write our paragraph about the doll just yet. The subject is too big. Let's write a paragraph about just the head of the doll.

We must put in order the parts of the head. Let's start at the top and work down again. This means we have to make another list of the parts of the head.

1. Hair
2. Eyes
4. Ears
5. Mouth

We have the order, the structure and enough material for a paragraph on the head.

STEP FOUR: Turn items into sentences.

We must write at least one sentence about each item of the head. Let's do that now.

1. Hair: *The hair is long and silky and has a slight curl in it.*
2. Eyes: *When the doll is turned on its back, the large, blue eyes close.*
3. Ears: *I know my doll can't hear me with its tiny ears, but I like to tell it secrets that I never would tell a real living person.*
4. Mouth: *There is always a smile on the lips.*

Day Three:

STEP FIVE: Write a topic sentence.

Once we have the body of our paragraph, we need an introduction to this group of sentences. This is called a **topic sentence**. This tells our reader what our paragraph will be about.

A topic sentence **introduces** our reader to the information in the paragraph. It also **limits** what we can talk about in our paragraph. If the topic sentence tells our reader that the doll costs a lot of money, then we can't talk about how beautiful the doll is. In that paragraph, we would have to talk about the cost of the doll.

In the body of the paragraph we're writing, we're talking about the head of our doll, so our topic sentence must introduce the head of the doll. Let's write our topic sentence.

The part of my doll I like best is the head.

STEP SIX: Put it all together.

We now have the whole paragraph about the head of the doll. I have numbered, made bold and underlined the parts of this example paragraph so you could see where those parts came from in the listing in **step four**.

(TS) *The part of my doll I like best is the head.* *(1)* *The hair is long and silky and has a slight curl in it.* *(2)* *When the doll is turned on its back, the large, blue eyes close.* *(3)* *I know my doll can't hear me with its tiny ears, but I like to tell it secrets that I never would tell a real, living person.* *(4)* *No matter what I say, there is always a smile on its lips.*

> **Hint: A well constructed paragraph can be a joy to read.**

WRITING

Day Four:

In the first three days you didn't have to write anything, but you know that'll change, right? You've learned that there are six steps to writing an organized paragraph. They are:

1. **Break the subject** into parts.
2. Put the parts into some **order.**
3. **Narrow** the topic.
4. Write **sentences** for the parts.
5. Write the **topic sentence.**
6. **Put it all together.**

If you've understood this, you're learning to think in an organized and adult way.

To write an organized paragraph, you have to pick a topic. This isn't a problem. I'll give you some suggestions:

1. My dog or cat
2. A new tool
3. My best friend
4. My room
5. The game I like to play best
6. The food I would rather not eat
7. My new bike (game, ball, pet or friend)

You're to use our six steps to write this paragraph. Do this writing on other paper. (But, try not to write about a doll.)

STEP ONE: Break the subject into parts.

Write the subject of your paragraph:_____

Write the parts this subject can be broken into. This can be physical or non-physical.

1. _____

2. _____

3. _____

4. _____

You don't have to use four parts, there can be three or five or eight. It depends on the subject and how you want to break it down.

STEP TWO: List the parts in order. Remember, you have a choice here.

On other paper, write the method you'll use to organize the parts: (*top to bottom, small to big and so on*)

_____

List again, on other paper, the parts but in the order you'll write about them:

1. _____

2. _____

3. _____

4. _____

If you can write a paragraph about any of the parts, then use that part as the topic of your paragraph, just as we did with the doll. If you do this, you should do step two over with a new list of parts for that point. If you don't do this, go on to step four.

STEP THREE: Narrow your topic: (*put new topic here*))_____

(Make new list if needed)

STEP FOUR: Make sentences out of the steps in the list:

1. _____

_____

2. _____

_____

3. _____

_____

STEP FIVE: Write the topic sentence. (Remember that it has to introduce what will be in the paragraph and it'll also limit what you can put in the paragraph to the subject of the topic sentence.)

_____

_____

_____

_____

You should set your paper up like the example below. Just before you hand it to your parent, check it against the example to be sure all the parts are where they should be.

You could title this paper "One Perfect Paragraph" and with pride, show it to your parent.

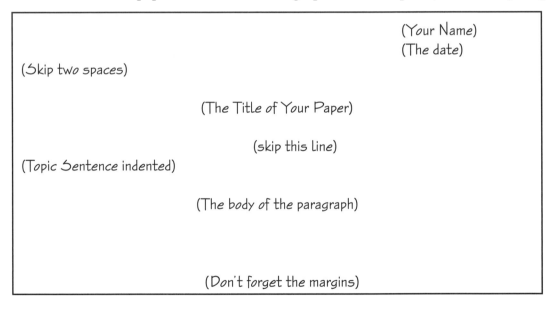

Hint: Go back and turn two of your sentences that are connected by subject into a compound sentence. Look up in your grammar text complex sentences and turn your compound sentence into a compound complex sentence.

Fill out the "Record of Progress" on the next page. I recommend you now take a week off from writing and concentrate on reading and discussing ideas with your parents.

RECORD OF PROGRESS

Name: _____ Date: _____

Exercise **#8 PARAGRAPHS**

This is the best sentence I wrote this week.

_____

_____

This mistake I made this week and I will not make it next week.

_____

_____

This is the sentence that had this mistake in it.

_____

_____

This is the sentence again showing how I fixed this mistake.

_____

_____

Comments:

#9 MY HOME (1)

SKILL: DESCRIPTION

It might take you six days to learn how to:
1. Understand the layout of a building
2. Show relationships of spaces in floor plans
3. Use a bird's-eye view
4. Create a drawing from what you see

PREWRITING

Days One and Two:

The three parts of the "My Home" exercise will teach you to write descriptions that are accurate. This is a very hard thing to do well. If you're careful with the work of the next few days, you should be able to do a good job writing descriptions.

In this part of the exercise, you're to make a floor plan (map) of your home. This means that when you're done, your floor plan will look like your home would look if some giant were to take off the roof and look straight down on it from high above, or if some bird were to look down on it. (That's where we get bird's eye view.) Your floor plan will have the kitchen, living room, bedrooms, den, closets and outside doors. Don't forget the bathroom and the hallways.

When you draw a bird's-eye view of a room, some of the things in the room shouldn't be drawn. For instance, the giant wouldn't be able to see the clocks or the pictures. She would be looking straight down. She'd be able to see the floors, the halls and the spaces where the doors are. So, that's all you should put in your floor plan. (A girl giant?)

How big the rooms are and how long and how wide the halls are isn't important. It won't be necessary to measure them. It would be good to try and make the relationships reasonable, though. Your parent may show you how to do this by pacing off a room in both directions. You'll see that the room is square or that it's longer in one way than it is in the other. In either case, your floor plan should show the relationships of the lengths to the widths for the rooms and the halls.

Of course, the hallway will be longer than it is wide. You may want to pace off the hall with your parent and ask to be shown on scrap paper the relationship of the length to the width of the area. While you're learning this, ask about the relationship of the size of your bedroom to the size of the hall outside your room. This will help you when you make your floor plan. Notice that the box below is about three times as long as it is wide. This is how you can talk about relationships of sizes.

WRITING

After your parent shows you how to figure relationships in size, take a trip through the house. Take paper and pencil. You'll need to make a rough sketch of where the doors and rooms are.

All maps and floor plans have north at the top of the page. If you're not sure about directions, have your parent show you which direction is north. The north side of the house should be at the top of your paper. Remember that moss grows on the north side of trees? That's how to tell directions in the woods. It doesn't work that way with rooms. There may be no moss it all on your house.

When making any map or writing descriptions, you should always start with general areas or statements first. So, the first things you should draw are the outside walls and the main rooms. (Remember you're looking down from high over your house.) This will let you see how the building is laid out. Your parent may pace off the rooms with you, and when you get back to your work area, your parent may show you how to figure how much larger some of the rooms are than others.

Day Three:

You should have a rough drawing of the outside walls and the positions of the outside doors. If you had trouble with this part, be sure and ask your parent to help you, because it'll be hard for you to continue if this isn't understood or done correctly. Now draw in the major room areas. When you get to the kitchen and pace it off, be sure to check for cookies.

Day Four:

Today you'll place the windows and inside doorways. Remember, you're looking down on the rooms, but it won't be necessary to draw in the tables and chairs.

Days Five and Six:

Using your sketch as a model, make a neat floor plan because you will be using it for the next two exercises. It would be good if you were to use a ruler to make straight lines. You'll want to write the name of the room in the center of each one. You should write the word "North" at the top of the page.

Fill out the "Record of Progress" on the next page. I recommend you now take a week off from writing and concentrate on reading and discussing ideas with your parents.

RECORD OF PROGRESS

Name: _____ Date: _____

Exercise **#9 MY HOME (1)**

This is the best sentence I wrote this week.

_____

_____

This mistake I made this week and I will not make it next week.

_____

_____

This is the sentence that had this mistake in it.

_____

_____

This is the sentence again showing how I fixed this mistake.

_____

_____

Comments:

#10 MY HOME (2)

SKILL: DESCRIPTION

It should take you five days to learn to:
1. Understand the structure of description
2. Describe a building starting with general statements
3. Support general statements with detail
4. Turn graphic representations into verbal descriptions (drawings into words)

PREWRITING

Day One:

In the last exercise you drew a floor plan of your home. This is one way of describing something. Now you'll describe your home using words. This time you'll not have to walk through the house. You'll be able to work from your floor plan.

Just as you started your floor plan with a general outline of the outside walls of the building, you'll start your description with general statements about the building.

(Do you need to read that last paragraph again?)

INTRODUCTION

Your parent will have to tell you a little of the information you will need for the **introduction** of your paper, for your **introduction** should include at least one sentence for each of the following:

1. The **name of your house or apartment** (The Smith House or The Smith Apartment)
2. **Where it's located** (The town it's in and the street it's on)
3. **When it was built**
4. **How many rooms** it has
5. **How many floors** it has
6. **How many people** live in it

WRITING

Day Two:
   BODY

The **first paragraph** of the **body** of your paper should contain the following:

1. A statement about the **shape and size** of your building or unit. When talking about shape, it might help your reader if you could describe the shape using shapes familiar to your reader: *My house is square* or *U shaped*, or *My house is L shaped.*

2. Your reader should be told about the **number of halls** there are and in which **direction they run.**

3. There should be a sentence that lists the **general areas** of the building and a statement about the **number of rooms** there are. This could sound like this:

   In my home there are a number of areas: a large living room area, a kitchen and eating area, a formal dining room, a study and school room for the kid's homeschooling, a den for my parents and a small garage.

4. Your reader should be told **where the major areas** in your home are. It might sound like this:

   On the north side of the house, the front door opens into a short entryway that is next to the living room. The kitchen and breakfast room are in the back of the house on the south side. The bedrooms are on the east end of the building. That is where the sun can wake us up all summer.

   DO NOT WRITE: *"When you walk in the front door. . ."* or, *"As you enter the den, on the right wall. . ."* You're **not** taking your reader on a tour of the house, just **describing it.**

Day Three:
   The **second paragraph** should describe the function of the rooms: (Who spends time in them and what's done in them)

1. **How the rooms are used.** It might read like this:

   The big living room is mostly reserved for company. It has light colored carpet in it and what we call "good furniture." When company comes or when we have a party at our house, we all use the living room.

49

2. The **bedrooms** part of your paper might read like this:

The master bedroom is where my parents sleep. Dad has an exercise bike in there but the kids aren't allowed to use it. My brother has the small bedroom on the north-east corner of the house and I have the one next to it on the east side of the house.

3. When you write about the total number of rooms there are in the building, you want to be sure you count the bathrooms and closets.

Day Four:
The **third paragraph of the body** should contain the following information:

1. **Where the closets are** in each of the rooms.
2. **Where the pantry or storage room is.**
3. **Where any special rooms are**. These could be rooms like the den, the laundry room or the play room in the basement.

Day Five:
CONCLUSION

This paper needs a **conclusion**. A conclusion should do a number of things:

1. **Tie all the ideas in the body together.** In this paper the ideas in the body are:

A. There are a lot of rooms in your home, and;

B. It was designed so that the owners would find it easy to use.

This part of the conclusion could sound like this:

This house was very well designed. It is an easy building for my family to use because the places where we spend most of our time are near the outside doors.

2. Make some **statement about what you think of your house**. It's not enough to say that you like it. What you say about your home must have something to do with the way it was designed and how it's used. This part could read this way:

My home is like a fort to me. When I'm home I feel really secure and safe. When I'm with my family and we watch television or listen to the radio, I'm always glad that I live in this house with these people. I often wish all kids could live in as good a place as my family has.

It would be really easy to do an exercise like this one where there are lots of examples that I've written for you, if you were to **use my sentence structuring and my wording**. But, you know that that wouldn't help you much. And besides, your parents won't let you get away with it. So, don't even try.

This chart will show you how to set up your paper.

```
                                                            (Your Name)
                                                            (The date)

(Skip two spaces)


                                 (My House)
(Skip one line and then skip no other lines)
(Introduction)




(Body)          (Do not label the parts of your paper nor skip lines
                between them)






(Conclusion)



(Make sure you have equal margins on all sides of your paper

                     (Page numbers bottom center)
```

> **Hint: Try to draw a floor plan of your house from your description of it.**

Fill out the "Record of Progress" on the next page. I recommend you now take a week off from writing and concentrate on reading and discussing ideas with your parents.

RECORD OF PROGRESS

Name: _____ Date: _____

Exercise **#10 MY HOME (2)**

This is the best sentence I wrote this week.

_____

_____

This mistake I made this week and I will not make it next week.

_____

_____

This is the sentence that had this mistake in it.

_____

_____

This is the sentence again showing how I fixed this mistake.

_____

_____

Comments:

#11 MY HOME (3)

SKILL: DESCRIPTION

It should take you just two days to learn:
1. That a description of a building should be good enough so that someone else can make a floor plan from it
2. That you can study your own work and decide if it needs to be changed or made better
3. That you can add to or change your writing to make it better

PREWRITING

Days One and Two:

You've studied your home. You've made a floor plan of it. You've described your home with words. Now's the time for you to find out how well you've done.

Your parent will give your "My Home (2)" paper to a neighbor or friend of the family. If this isn't possible, your parent might ask some family member to help. This person will use your word description of your house to try to draw a floor plan from it. The helper will be told not to draw a floor plan from what that person remembers about your house. Only your descriptions may be used.

If your description doesn't tell where something goes, it can be put anywhere. If you weren't very careful with your description, you might get a floor plan back that was based on your description that has the kitchen in the middle of the living room.

It should take only a short time for your description and the new floor plan to get back to you. There will be lots to do while you wait.

> **Hint: Neat's not bad.**

When you get your description back, it'll have a floor plan stapled to it, and if it doesn't look like the floor plan you drew for the "My Home (1)" exercise, that might mean that you made a mistake in the writing. Of course, the neighbor who made a floor plan from your description might not have known how draw a floor plan from a description.

(You could try to use this as an excuse, but I don't recommend it.)

WRITING

When you get your paper back, you'll have to do one of the following two things:

1. You'll have to write an explanation to your parent of why there's a difference between the floor plan the neighbor drew from your description and the way your home really is; or,

2. You'll have to explain to your parent how come you did everything just right so that the neighbor could draw a floor plan that looks just the way your house really is.

If you have to do #1, you should:

A. Write a paper that describes where the problem is in your "My Home (2)" paper.

B. Add to or change the wording in your paper so the neighbor could draw a good floor plan from it.

If you have to do #2, you should:

A. Describe the steps you took to do a perfect job.

B. Describe how hard you worked.

C. Talk to your parent about more cookies.

I want you to know that this kind of an exercise is really hard. I've given work like this to many high school kids and every year some of them had trouble with it. This doesn't mean they're dumb or poor students. This kind of thinking was just not their style. It's like me and dancing. I've never been able to feel music enough to learn to dance. I've felt bad about that, but I know that's just the way I am. If you had lots of trouble with this exercise, that's okay. You should get cookies anyway.

> **Hint: You even could send me one.**

Fill out the "Record of Progress" on the next page. I recommend you now take a week off from writing and concentrate on reading and discussing ideas with your parents.

RECORD OF PROGRESS

Name: _____ Date: _____

Exercise **#11 MY HOME (3)**

This is the best sentence I wrote this week.

_____

_____

This mistake I made this week and I will not make it next week.

_____

_____

This is the sentence that had this mistake in it.

_____

_____

This is the sentence again showing how I fixed this mistake.

_____

_____

Comments:

PROBLEMS I HAVE SOLVED THIS FIRST SEMESTER

1. _____

_____

2. _____

_____

3. _____

_____

4. _____

_____

5. _____

_____

6. _____

_____

7. _____

_____

8. _____

_____

How I feel about this progress I'm making:

_____

_____

#12 DESCRIBING A THOUGHT PROBLEM

SKILL: ORGANIZATION

It may take you three days to learn to:
1. Picture a situation in your mind which would be a problem
2. Describe what such an imaginary situation would be like
3. Solve a thought problem

PREWRITING

Days One through Three:

Describing a thing isn't too hard because you can look at it and say what it looks like. If it's small enough, you can even pick it up and describe what it feels like and tell how heavy it is. Think of model cars and oranges.

What's hard to do is to describe a problem. That's why it's so much fun. It's no fun to do easy things. Anyone can do them. We'll work together on a thought problem, and then maybe your parent will let you work on one by yourself.

Let's start our problem with the words, **what if**. Now all we have to do is think of a problem and introduce it with those words. Here are some possibilities.

1. **What if** there were no more books?
2. **What if** one morning none of the engines in any of the cars, trucks, or buses would run?
3. **What if** one day people had no thumbs?
4. **What if** all the people in the world woke up one morning and they were all the same color?
5. **What if** people or cats or dogs could fly?

There's no end to the possibilities for thought problems. It gets fun to think of all the things that would have to change or be done with some of the *what if* problems. I'll choose a problem and we'll work through it together.

What if, one morning, the public library were floating two feet off the ground?

That's crazy isn't it? But, that's why it's fun. The first thing we'll have to do is describe what the building would look like floating in the air, and then we'll have to solve the problems this would cause. So, this exercise will have two parts:

Part 1. Describe a thought problem as if it were real

Part 2. Solve the thought problem

To do this we'll have to:

1. **See the floating library** in our minds
2. **Describe** in detail what we see
3. Tell what the **people would do** in this situation
4. Decide how the **people could solve** the problem
5. **Describe the solving** of the problem

Very few buildings float, so we'll have to be creative and use our imaginations.

We'll write this in **past tense**, except for the **last sentence** which will be in the **present tense.** (Read that sentence again.) I'm going to write the whole exercise as an example just as if I were doing it, because I really like thought problems.

The Floating Library

When we went to the library on Monday morning to get more books for reading in our homeschool, the building was floating two feet off the ground. Even the front lawn, the sidewalks and the night depository stand were floating. Kids were jumping off the lawn onto the street and then climbing back up onto the library property. Some of the librarians were having trouble clambering up onto the high sidewalks.

When the head librarian came to work, he put a box on the edge of the walk so others could get into the building. The mayor came in a police car to find out what all the excitement was about. That afternoon she called a meeting of the city council to see what could be done about the floating library.

The mayor and the council invited anyone who wanted to come to the meeting to do so and tell what they thought could be done to get the building back down. The mayor and all the important people in town decided that the library was too light and that was why it was floating. They thought that if they made the building darker it might settle back down. They painted all the windows with black paint. As soon as this was done the library started to lower. When the mayor told the head librarian to turn off all the lights in the building, the library dropped down with a plop.

The mayor explained the problem in the paper the next day. She said that the library had too much light reading in it. She told the head librarian to order some heavy reading. She said that when this was done it would anchor the building and give it a good foundation.

Once the problem was solved, we could go back to the library to read and get books. Only now the books are so heavy, we have to take a wheelbarrow to bring any home, and, if we want to read the books there, we have to take a flashlight.

You should recognize that some of the words I chose were used in a punning way. Puns use words that have two meanings. See if you can spot them and tell your parent how I distorted the ideas in the writing by using puns.

Don't just read that last paragraph—do it. That's what this writing program is all about, getting you to think and put your thoughts together so other people can understand what you really mean. Looking for puns can help or I wouldn't have suggested it. (*So, do it.*)

WRITING

Start your mind working on the *What if* sentence. If you can't think of one, use one of my suggestions listed on the first page of this exercise. As soon as you've selected a problem, picture it in your mind; then you'll be ready to write.

Use this outline to help you organize your thinking:

1. **Describe the problem** in **past tense.**
2. Tell how the **people acted**.
3. Tell how **they tried to solve** the problem.
4. Explain how the **problem was solved.**
5. Tell **what it's like <u>now</u>** after the problem **has been** solved. (Use **present tense** for this last step.)

The chart on the next page might be of some help.

> **Hint: When you pick a thought problem, don't hold back. Make it fun.**

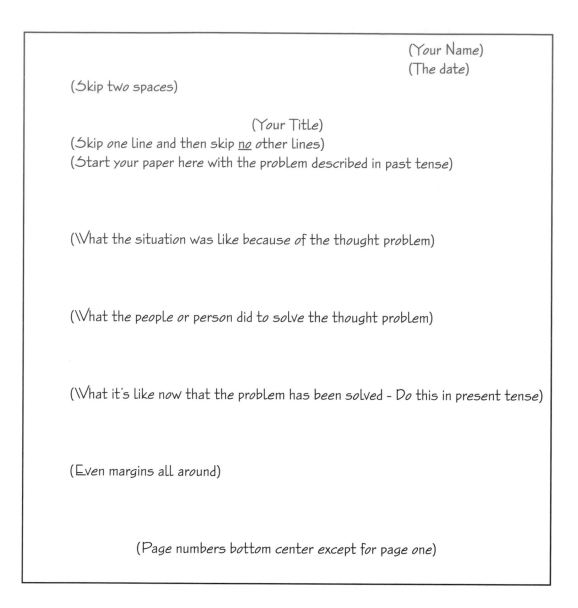

(Your Name)
(The date)

(Skip two spaces)

(Your Title)
(Skip one line and then skip <u>no</u> other lines)
(Start your paper here with the problem described in past tense)

(What the situation was like because of the thought problem)

(What the people or person did to solve the thought problem)

(What it's like now that the problem has been solved - Do this in present tense)

(Even margins all around)

(Page numbers bottom center except for page one)

Before you start writing the final copy of this exercise, check this chart to make sure your paper will be set up this way.

> **Hint: Don't give your parents your paper until you're proud of it.**

Fill out the "Record of Progress" on the next page. I recommend you now take a week off from writing and concentrate on reading and discussing ideas with your parents.

RECORD OF PROGRESS

Name: _____ Date: _____

Exercise **#12 DESCRIBING A THOUGHT PROBLEM**

This is the best sentence I wrote this week.

_____

_____

This mistake I made this week and I will not make it next week.

_____

_____

This is the sentence that had this mistake in it.

_____

_____

This is the sentence again showing how I fixed this mistake.

_____

_____

Comments:

#13 PERSON

SKILL: BASIC

It might take you four days to learn to:
1. Use first person
2. Use third person
3. Avoid careless use of second person
4. Control the use of person in your writing

PREWRITING

Days One and Two:

A writer, creating a narrative voice which speaks to the reader, must select what we call *person*. This is the name given to one characteristic of the voice the writer uses to tell the story. There are three forms (called *number*) of this voice. Your parent may want to read to you the following examples and go over them with you. If this isn't clear, read this paragraph again and then ask your parent to explain it to you. This is important.

1. **First person** (using **I or we**) sounds like this: *I (we) saw the car when it came toward the crossroad.* First person reads like the voice is part of the action.

2. **Second person** (using **you**) sounds like this: *When you stood on the corner, you saw the car as it came at you.* Second person makes the reader part of the story.

3. **Third person** (using **he, she** or **they**) sounds like this: *He was standing on the corner when the car came toward the intersection.* The use of third person puts the narrative voice outside of the story. It makes the voice a non-part of the action. The narrative voice becomes just a teller of the story.

You must be careful when you write not to change the form (number) of your narrative voice. When I explained something to the students I had in my classes, they sometimes forgot what they had heard. They tried, but it was hard for them to do everything right. It may take practice for you to remember to control your use of person.

Read over the last paragraph again. Notice that there's the use of the words *you* and *they,* but this doesn't mean I'm using the second or third person. My narrative voice is still talking in **first person, using I.** In this example the voice (in first person) is using *you* and *they* to refer to other characters. Make sure that this is clear to you before you go on. You might want to discuss this with your parent.

WRITING

Today you'll practice using **third** person by writing a paragraph of directions written in **third person, using *he, she* or *they.*** This will be hard because you'll want to use **second person,** *you*. ***Don't***. You're going to describe how to do something. It'll be easier if you tell how to do something that's simple.

A good way to start when faced with the job of describing to another person how to do something, is to make a list of steps or procedures. These steps should be listed in the same order in which they should be done. There should be at least **eight steps** in your list. This list can be just words if you want it that way. Below is an example of what I mean by a list of steps for an example paragraph we'll write together. We might even give it a title:

How to Sharpen a Pencil

1. Face sharpener
2. Hold pencil in left hand, the end to be sharpened pointed to the right
3. Grasp handle on the right side of the sharpener with thumb and forefinger
4. Insert end of pencil in hole in top of the left end of sharpener
5. Turn crank clockwise facing right end of sharpener
6. Push on pencil while turning crank
7. Remove pencil and examine for sharpness (Repeat steps 4, 5 and 6 if necessary.)
8. Blow dust off sharpened end

Our next step is to turn our list into sentences in which the narrative voice uses **third person.** To make this example a paragraph, we'll have to have a topic sentence. The following sentence should work as a topic sentence. If we put this sentence before the directions, we'll have a fully developed paragraph.

Sharpening a pencil is an easy thing for a person to do.

> **Hint: Try to identify the person you're speaking in when you're in conversation with members of your family. Let them know you're doing this, and do it aloud.**

How to Sharpen a Pencil

*Sharpening a pencil is an easy thing for a **person** to do. A **boy** who would like to do this faces the sharpener. **He** then holds **his** pencil in **his** left hand so that the end to be sharpened points to **his** right. Using **his** right hand, **he** holds the handle on the right side of the sharpener with **his** thumb and forefinger. With **his** left hand **he** inserts the end of **his** pencil in the hole in the top of the left end of the sharpener.*

*   **He** turns the crank in a clockwise direction as **he** faces the right end of the sharpener and at the same time pushes the pencil into the sharpener. After a few turns of the handle, **he** removes **his** pencil and checks for sharpness. If it is not sharp enough, **he** repeats steps four, five and six. When the pencil is sharp, **he** blows the dust off the end that has been sharpened.*

Now it's your turn. You're to write a description in third person, just as we wrote how to sharpen a pencil in third person. (Try not to write about how to sharpen a pencil.)

Day Three:

Today you're to write the <u>**same directions**</u> that you wrote in the last two days, but this time they should be in **second person, using** *you*. This is the voice with which the writer talks directly to the reader and calls the reader *you*. This should sound like this:

*   **You** are holding **your** pencil in **your** left hand, pointing the end to be sharpened to **your** right.*

Notice that the narrative voice in this example speaks in **present tense**. You might want to try this in your paragraph.

Day Four:

You wrote directions in **third person**, **using** *he*, then the same directions in **second person, using** *you*. Today you'll write the same directions in first person, using *I*. This is the choice in which the narrative voice talks about itself. This should sound like this:

*   **I hold** the pencil in **my** left hand with the end to be sharpened pointing to **my** right.*

In this exercise, you should have learned to control use of the person of your narrative voice. Your parent may ask you explain these three voices to one of your other family members. (If you're not asked to do this, do it anyway. It's good for you.)

Fill out the "Record of Progress" on the next page. I recommend you now take a week off from writing and concentrate on reading and discussing ideas with your parents.

RECORD OF PROGRESS

Name: _____ Date: _____

Exercise **#13 PERSON**

This is the best sentence I wrote this week.

_____

_____

This mistake I made this week and I will not make it next week.

_____

_____

This is the sentence that had this mistake in it.

_____

_____

This is the sentence again showing how I fixed this mistake.

_____

_____

Comments:

#14 PAST, PRESENT AND FUTURE

SKILL: BASIC

You'll spend a number of days learning to control your use of:
1. Past tense
2. Present tense
3. Future tense

PREWRITING

Days One and Two:

To show how tenses work, I wanted to use a story as an example that everyone is familiar with and has a character we all know. I chose the wolf in the "Three Little Pigs." This wolf isn't very bright. In fact, he's a pretty dumb wolf. He tries to get at the pigs by blowing on their houses.

This is not a thinking animal. In most versions of this story, the narrative voice doesn't show the wolf thinking at all. But, that wolf must have some idea about what's going on. In a moment I'll show you what's going on in the wolf's mind.

(Notice that when I talk about what happens in a story I use present tense? This isn't logical, but remember, the rules of writing say it must be done.)

Your parent will select a short story for you. It should be written in past tense. You're to work with a number of pages in it from a point selected by your parent. You're to make a character think. Even if the author has the main character thinking in the story your parent selects for you, add to the thoughts the main character has.

Remember, the character's thoughts should be consistent with what you know about that character. If you recognize that character to be kind and gentle, that character's thoughts should be kind and gentle. (If this isn't clear, ask your parent for help.)

You should be aware that people think in all tenses. This is what it looks like when a character thinks in **past tense:**

Late in the afternoon, when the pains of hunger drove the wolf to seek his dinner, he saw three small houses in the valley. He thought, "Those three little houses that I saw yesterday were just like these and they were made by pigs. Maybe those pigs built houses that weren't strong."

This is what it looks like when a character thinks in **present tense:**

The wolf saw smoke coming from the chimney of the first house. He thought, "This house appears to be made of straw, and I'm standing out here and that pig is sitting in there, and we're both thinking about dinner!"

This is what it looks like when a character thinks in **future tense:**

The wolf began to drool, which made it hard for him to blow very hard. He kept having to spit. But, he did manage to take in a great lung-full of air. As he did this, he thought, "I'll have to keep my eyes peeled for that little porker. When this house goes, my dinner sure will be running for safety."

WRITING

For practice, on another piece of paper, for another part of this famous story, write some of the wolf's thoughts in **past tense.** (Use the sentence starts below.)

As the walls of the straw house began to lean away from the wolf, and the roof began to lift, the wolf thought,

Write the wolf's thoughts in **present tense:**

The wolf's hay fever got the best of him and he began to sneeze just as the house began to fall. When he took in a large breath, the house leaned toward him, and when he sneezed, it leaned away. He had to hold his nose to keep the straw dust out of it. He thought,

Write the wolf's thoughts in **future tense:**

When the straw house finally fell in and the dust cleared, the wolf stepped into the rubble looking for his ham dinner. The pig was not there! Wiping the tears from his eyes, he thought,

Day Three to the End of the Exercise:
Finish the story your parent chose for you from the spot your parent selected. Make sure your character thinks in all three tenses.

Set your paper up as this example demonstrates.

(Your Name)
(The date)

(Skip two spaces)

13 Past, Present and Future

(Skip one line)
(Story title)
(Character's name)
(Pages used and how)

Character's thoughts in past tense:

Character's thoughts in present tense:

Character's thoughts in future tense:

(Except for first page, page numbers bottom center)

Hint: A quotation within a quotation gets one quote mark. (Bill said, "John said, 'Hi.'")

Fill out the "Record of Progress" on the next page. I recommend you now take a week off from writing and concentrate on reading and discussing ideas with your parents.

RECORD OF PROGRESS

Name: _____ Date: _____

Exercise **#14 PAST, PRESENT AND FUTURE**
This is the best sentence I wrote this week.

_____

_____

This mistake I made this week and I will not make it next week.

_____

_____

This is the sentence that had this mistake in it.

_____

_____

This is the sentence again showing how I fixed this mistake.

_____

_____

Comments:

#15 THINGS CHANGE

SKILL: DESCRIPTION

It may take you seven days to learn that:
1. Things do change
2. Descriptions of changes can be organized
3. You can describe changes so they are easy to understand

PREWRITING

Day One:

As an example of how objects change, think of a peach. Before it's picked, it's small, hard and light green in color. When it's ripe enough to be picked, it's full of juice, bright yellow and peach colored, and soft. When it's been sitting on a shelf for two weeks, it has large, brown rotten spots on it. Its skin has begun to dry and wrinkle.

For this exercise you'll have to ask your parent or the produce man at the grocery store to sell you two pieces of fruit. One fresh and one which is starting to rot. You'll describe these two pieces of fruit as if they were the same piece but examined at different times:

First description: When it's ready to eat

Second description: After it's been sitting on a shelf too long

You'll need an **introduction** for this paper. In some introductions you can use an experience you've had that caused you to think about the subject.

Your **introduction for this paper will have three parts:**

1. **An experience** that started you thinking about how some things change

2. **A decision** to examine change in an organized way

3. **A mention of the object** you used to examine the ways things change

We haven't written an introduction like this one before, so it might help you to have more explanation. In this introduction you'll write about the above three things. Below is a short list of possibilities for the first point. Let's use #1 and I'll show you how it could be used and how to organize your introduction. (This means that you can't use my wording or situation in your paper.)

First point for the introduction:

My father and I stopped at our minister's house to wish him a happy birthday. He was in the garden pulling weeds. We stood at one end of a row of sweet corn and talked to him for a few minutes. I was impressed with how dirty his clothes were. His knees had dark patches of dirt on them and his shirt was dirty where he had wiped his face against it clearing the sweat out of his eyes. This is the first time I had ever seen him when he wasn't neat and clean.

Second point for the introduction:

I was so impressed by this change in his appearance that I thought about how all things must change, and I decided to look at the process of change. But, I knew I wouldn't understand much about change unless I made an organized examination.

Third point for the introduction:

I chose to examine a peach and watch it as it rotted. I set one on the windowsill in the kitchen and took notes as it rotted.

(These three points of the introduction will be in one paragraph, but it won't have a topic sentence.)

For your introduction, here are some things you could notice that would make you want to examine the change in the fruit. Most things are almost always the same, think of a situation where there might be a great change in appearance:

1. Your minister/priest/rabbi is always dressed up and clean. (You can't use it now)
2. Your grocery store manager always wears shoes.
3. Your neighborhood fire truck is always polished.
4. The electricity in the library always works.
5. The halls in your hospital are always clean and shiny.

> **Hint: If you're wonderful now, don't change.**

Review: If you can't think of a situation, you may pick one of the above examples. Begin your introduction by telling your reader that you had an experience where something had changed. This made you realize that many things can change in appearance. To study this idea, you took a piece of fruit and examined it at different times to see the progression of changes in physical characteristics.

WRITING

Start your introduction. Make sure your parent has a chance to read it before you're done studying writing for today.

Homework:

("HOMEWORK?!") How could you have homework if all of your school work is done at home? What else could I call it? *Schoolwork? Outside work? After-home work?* I can't think of anything else to call it but homework. No! Let's call it *preparation.* So, for your preparation, rewrite your introduction using the suggestions your parent has given you.

(This means that after your schooling day is completed, you should do the preparation for the next day's lesson.)

Day Two:

When you describe how something's changed, you can write about how it looks and how it feels. In this case you probably won't want to describe how the rotten fruit tastes.

When you write about how the fruit looks, you can write about:

1. Color   3. Shape
2. Size   4. Texture

When you write about how the fruit feels, (Not sad or lonely) you can write about:

1. Smoothness
2. Wetness or dryness
3. Softness or firmness
4. Weight

Today you'll write about how the fresh fruit looks. There should be at least two or three sentences about each of the conditions in the above list on appearance.

Preparation: (Again?)

Using your parent's suggestions, you should rewrite your paragraph about how the fresh fruit looks and prepare it to show your parent on day three.

Day Three:

Write about how the fresh fruit feels. Again, there should be at least two or three sentences about each of the conditions in the list of how things feel.

Preparation: (Is there no end to this?!)

You should use your parent's suggestions and rewrite your paragraph about how the fresh fruit feels and prepare it to show to your parent for day four.

Day Four:

You will write about how the rotten fruit looks. Your parent will give you suggestions about how to improve your work.

Preparation: (Whew!)

Rewrite your paragraph about how the rotten fruit looks and prepare it to show it to your parent on day five.

Day Five:

Write the paragraphs about how the rotten fruit feels.

Preparation: (Not again!?!)

Rewrite your paragraphs about how the rotten fruit feels.

Day Six:

Your **conclusion** should have three points as listed below:

Point 1. You might mention the **observation** which **caused** you to think about how things change. (Don't write the whole thing over again)

Point 2. You should tell your reader **what you've learned** about organizing your description of things now that you've learned that change is normal.

Point 3. You might mention that **now you'll be looking** for signs of change.

Conclusions are harder to write than are introductions. I'll demonstrate how to write one using the above three points.

EXAMPLE CONCLUSION:

Point 1. *I'm surprised when I think that this whole examination started with my minister weeding his corn.* **Point 2.** *But, I'm glad we stopped by on his birthday, because I ended up learning a lot about the need to organize my thinking when I want to find out about things.* **Point 3.** *I realize from this that almost everything changes, I'll watch for signs of this everywhere now.*

(One of the problems with my writing examples for you is that you can't use my wording in your papers. You can use the structure of the paragraphs, though.)

Preparation: (Finally, this is it)

Prepare your whole paper to present it to your parent on day seven. Use this chart.

```
                                                        (Your Name)
                                                        (The date)

   (Skip two spaces)
                                    (Your Title)
   (Skip one line)
   INTRODUCTION
    Point 1
    Point 2
    Point 3              (Skip no line here)
   BODY
   Fresh Fruit
       Looks
       Feels
   Rotten Fruit
       Looks
       Feels             (Skip no line here)
   CONCLUSION
    Point 1
    Point 2
    Point 3
                    (Page numbers bottom center)
```

Fill out the "Record of Progress" on the next page. I recommend you now take a week off from writing and concentrate on reading and discussing ideas with your parents.
:

RECORD OF PROGRESS

Name: _____ Date: _____

Exercise **#15 THINGS CHANGE**
This is the best sentence I wrote this week.

_____

_____

This mistake I made this week and I will not make it next week.

_____

_____

This is the sentence that had this mistake in it.

_____

_____

This is the sentence again showing how I fixed this mistake.

_____

_____

Comments:

#16 FROM WHERE I WAS

SKILL: CREATION

It may take you five days to learn that:
1. Characters in fiction must be in specific places
2. Position (place) determines what characters can experience
3. You can control the position of your first person narrative voice characters

PREWRITING

Day One:
When the narrative voice is a character speaking in first person, that character/voice has to be in some real place in the story.

(Read that sentence again and again until you're sure you understand exactly what it means.)

This narrative voice position determines what that character/narrative voice can see and understand about the action that takes place.

You're to write two accounts of the same event. Both of them will be in **first person** but the first in **past** and the second in **present** tense. Your parent may want to discuss this idea with you and read through the rest of this exercise with you.

Your paper will have, as narrative voices, different characters in the same action. If you follow this outline, it may help you write **these two views** of the action. Your paper should contain:

1. **The positions of the characters** in your action
2. **A scenario** of the event (This should be in third person and in present tense.)
3. **The first account** of the event as told by one of the characters in past tense
4. **The second account** of the same event as told by another character in present tense

> **Hint: Think of yourself as a character in a piece of fiction. What can you know from where you are?**

#1. CHARACTER POSITIONS

Character A. *Bill is in the back of the garage looking behind the bench for a wrench to use to tighten the hose on the faucet at the side of the house.*

Character B. *Janet is in the old refrigerator box she has turned into a large dollhouse. She can see out a small window she has cut in the side of the box.*

Character C. *Mr. Roberts has backed the family station wagon up to the garage and is unloading it.*

#2. SCENARIO   (All scenarios are written in present tense.)

It is Bill's birthday and Mr. Roberts has bought Bill a new ten-speed mountain bike. He backs the family station wagon up to the garage and looks around the yard to be sure that Bill won't see him unload the bike.

Janet is in her refrigerator-box dollhouse and watches her father unload a new blue bike from the car. She has seen Bill come into the garage but does not know if he has seen their father with the bike and says nothing.

Bill has heard the car drive up, but he is looking for a wrench he has dropped behind the work bench at the back of the garage, and, looking upside down at the world, sees a bike being unloaded.

#3. FIRST ACCOUNT— JANET:

I was fixing my dollhouse when I heard Bill come into the garage. I knew it was him 'cause I could hear his whistling. Nobody whistles the way Bill does; there's no tune at all. He just makes this whistling sound between his teeth, both in and out. It really gets on my nerves sometimes.

He was in the back of the garage and Dad backed up to the door with the car and unloaded a new bike. It was just what Bill's been asking for. I watched out the window I cut in the box. I don't think anybody knew I was there at all.

#4. SECOND ACCOUNT— BILL:

I have to find a wrench to tighten the hose on the faucet. Dad doesn't like it to drip and run down the driveway. I know Janet is in the box in the garage as soon as I walk in. I can hear her talking to her dolls. I start that whistling I know bugs her just to let her know I know she is there. Just as I find the wrench, I drop it behind the bench, and, at the same time, Dad backs the car up to the garage. He gets out and looks around like he is afraid of being seen. I have to look at all this between the shelves and hanging upside-down, because I am leaning over the back of the bench reaching down trying to get my fingers on the wrench. I don't think he even sees me. Then he unloads the neatest bike! It is all I can do not to yell out.

77

WRITING

Day Two:

Step #1. Create the position of your characters. You'll have to plan what you're going to write about before you do this. You may use any incident you like. (Look at my example step #1 on the first page of this exercise)

You should ask your parent to read what you've written before the end of this day's work.

Day Three:

Step #2. It may take two days to write the scenario. When you have a rough draft finished, ask your parent to look over your work. (Before you start, check my example scenario)

Day Four:

Step #3. Write the first account of the event as told in first person and **past tense** by one of the characters. When you have the rough draft finished, ask your parent to give you suggestions.

Preparation: (See how nicely this word works?)

Rewrite your rough draft using your parent's suggestions and turn it in on day five.

Day Five:

Step #4. Write the second account as told by another character in first person and in **present tense**

Preparation:

Rewrite the second account so you can give your parent the finished paper on day six.

> **Hint: Who says you're not wonderful?**

Fill out the "Record of Progress" on the next page. I recommend you now take a week off from writing and concentrate on reading and discussing ideas with your parents.

RECORD OF PROGRESS

Name: _____ Date: _____

Exercise **#16 FROM WHERE I WAS**

This is the best sentence I wrote this week.

_____

_____

This mistake I made this week and I will not make it next week.

_____

_____

This is the sentence that had this mistake in it.

_____

_____

This is the sentence again showing how I fixed this mistake.

_____

_____

Comments:

#17 ATTITUDE IN DESCRIPTION

SKILL: DESCRIPTION

It may take you eight days to learn that:
1. Authors give attitudes to their narrative voices
2. You can give your reader feelings by the attitudes you give your first-person characters

PREWRITING

Day One:

One of the major jobs authors have is controlling the feelings of their readers. There are many ways authors do this, and one of the easiest to understand is to examine the ways they describe objects and situations.

In this paper you'll describe a situation **two times**.

The **first** time you'll make your reader **like it.**
The **second** time you'll make your reader **dislike it.**

First description: You'll write about a picnic as if you're a mother who loves all kids. You must make your reader enjoy all of the things the mother sees, hears and smells. If you use the following list it may help: (Don't start writing yet)

She Sees:
1. The bright colors of the clothing
2. The fast movements of the excited kids
3. The fixing and eating of hot dogs and desserts
4. The laughing and smiling faces
5. The eagerness of the kids to be together
6. The fun the kids have running and playing
7. The other mothers laughing and talking with the kids

She Hears:
1. The loud laughter and talking
2. The rustle and pop of paper bags and pop cans
3. The bang and crash of silverware
4. The noise of speedboats on the lake

She Smells:
1. The pickles and mustard
2. The charcoal fire and the broiling hot dogs
3. The orange and red pop

WRITING

Today you'll write about what the mother sees. Be sure your parent reads what you've written before the end of the work for today. This should be written in first person and in present tense. (If you've forgotten how this works, check exercise #7.)

The example below illustrates how it's possible to show how a character might be feeling about an event or a place:

Standing at the end of the slide helping some of the younger children, I've forgotten my own. I look up and the picnic area is just a sea of color. There are kids everywhere. Now, what color is Bill's shirt? I think it's blue. There must be hundreds of boys with blue on.
A speeding boat near the beach creates white waves that wash over the swimming children and my eyes shoot to the water. Has he gone swimming? Is he out too far—in danger from the boat? I look around, frantic now, for my child. And see him by the table of food. I should have known where he'd be.

Preparation: (I'm so proud of this word.)

Finish your rough draft of what the mother sees for day two. Remember that your reader should feel that the mother likes what she's seeing and so should the reader.

Day Two:

While your parent reads the completed rough draft of the first section, you'll write about what the mother hears. The mother and reader should like what she hears.

Preparation:

Show your parent on day three:
1. A finished copy of what the mother sees
2. A rough draft of what the mother hears

Day Three:

Write the piece on what the mother smells. Keep in mind that the mother likes what she sees, hears and smells and so should the reader.

Preparation:

Show your parent on day four:
1. The finished copy of what the mother hears
2. The completed rough draft of what the mother smells

Day Four:

Today you'll have a chance to catch up on your writing. You should have finished copies of all three pieces by day five. Have your parent look over what you've prepared.

Days Five through Eight:

Second description: You have a chance to write about the picnic as if it were being described by the grounds keeper who has to clean up after the picnic. You should use the same list, except the man will look, hear and smell things differently from how the mother does. This section should also be in first person and in present tense. You'll have four days to write this. You'll want to have your parent look over your rough drafts before you write your final copies. (Your reader should understand that the man doesn't like what he sees, hears and smells and neither should the reader.)

This example may help you to get started:

What a mess. It looks like there's a war going on here. Paper, garbage, pop cans and even a pair of shoes—and half the stuff's in the air, being thrown. I don't know why these mothers can't clean up after their own kids. Even catsup on the swings! And half the paper bags and wax paper they brought here are on the ground, blowing in the wind. What a job.

Day Eight:

At the end of today's lesson you should have a final copy (revised and clean) of the two pieces.

> **Hint: If you're not proud of what you've written, take another day and make it better. Always turn in to others only your best work.**

Fill out the "Record of Progress" on the next page. I recommend you now take a week off from writing and concentrate on reading and discussing ideas with your parents.

RECORD OF PROGRESS

Name: _____ Date: _____

Exercise **#17 ATTITUDE IN DESCRIPTION**

This is the best sentence I wrote this week.

_____

_____

This mistake I made this week and I will not make it next week.

_____

_____

This is the sentence that had this mistake in it.

_____

_____

This is the sentence again showing how I fixed this mistake.

_____

_____

Comments:

#18 THE LONG AND SHORT OF IT

SKILL: CREATION

It may take you three days to learn that:
1. Sentence length is important
2. You can control the length of your sentences to help your reader appreciate and understand what you have to say

PREWRITING

Days One and Two:

When you talk to your friends, all of the sentences you use are not of the same length. This is because you already understand how the length of your sentences can help your friends understand what you're saying. If you were telling your friend about a car crash, you would automatically change the lengths of your sentences. This example will convince you that you do this. You might structure your sentences this way:

We were headed downtown. Me and my brother heard this siren when we got to the corner at Main Street.

We were on the sidewalk by the drug store and here comes this cop car. This old Buick is just starting out from the stop street when he sees the flashing lights. He slams on the brakes. This guy behind him doesn't see him stop and bangs into him, hard. Crash! Boy, was that a mess, with glass all over.

This is the way people talk and that's the way good writers write dialogue. I tried to make this conversation sound real, and then I counted the words. This is what I found:

Paragraph, sentence number and sentence length:

Paragraph I	Paragraph II	
Sentence 1. 4 words	Sentence 1. 15 words	5. 1 word
2. 16 words	2. 17 words	6. 9 words
	3. 5 words	
	4. 13 words	

84

WRITING

You'll write about an event. It should be written in third person and past tense. Put dialogue in it which should sound like real people talking. This means that the sentences must be of different lengths.

An easy way to practice this is to create two people in conversation and have one of them be an adult and one of them be a kid. You could write about a mother asking her son about cleaning his room. Or you could write about a young girl telling her mother what she wants for Christmas. (You'll have to have the characters give fairly long speeches in order to give you an opportunity to vary the lengths of their sentences.)

Day Three:

Today you're to finish your writing and then count the lengths of the sentences in your paper. If you find your sentences are different in length by only one or two words, you should rewrite some of them. Include this analysis in your final paper. See the example.

Ask your parent to look at your work each day and suggest how to improve it. Your parent may want you to write a final copy. This means that it'll be neat and have no spelling or punctuation errors in it.

This is a short exercise but it's an important one. You should practice using different length sentences even when you're describing things or writing letters to your friends. They'll enjoy your letters more. And so will you. Every time you write, think about sentence length variety. (If you're a short person, that's something else entirely.)

You could set your paper up this way:

```
                                                    (Your Name and the date)
        (Skip two spaces)


                          (The Title of Your Paper)
        (Skip one line)
        (The conversation)
        (Skip two spaces)
        (The sentence length analysis)



                          (Page numbers bottom center)
```

Fill out the "Record of Progress" on the next page. I recommend you now take a week off from writing and concentrate on reading and discussing ideas with your parents.

RECORD OF PROGRESS

Name: _____ Date: _____

Exercise **#18 THE LONG AND SHORT OF IT**

This is the best sentence I wrote this week.

_____

_____

This mistake I made this week and I will not make it next week.

_____

_____

This is the sentence that had this mistake in it.

_____

_____

This is the sentence again showing how I fixed this mistake.

_____

_____

Comments:

PROBLEMS I HAVE SOLVED THIS SECOND SEMESTER

1. _____

_____

2. _____

_____

3. _____

_____

4. _____

_____

5. _____

_____

6. _____

_____

7. _____

_____

8. _____

_____

How I feel about this progress I'm making:

_____

_____

COMMON PROBLEMS
with DEFINITIONS * RULES * EXAMPLES

AMBIGUITY

A statement may be taken in two ways.

1. She saw the man walking down the street.

> This can mean either:
> A. *She saw the man when **she** was walking down the street; or,*
> B. *She saw the man when **he** was walking down the street.*

2. The use of pronouns it, she, they, them that do not have clear antecedents (what they refer to) can create ambiguous sentences:

> *Bill looked at the coach when <u>he</u> got the money.*

> This can mean either:
> A. *When Bill got the money **he** looked at the coach; or,*
> B. *Bill looked at him when **the coach** got the money.*

APOSTROPHE

An apostrophe (') is a mark used to indicate possession or contraction.

Rules:

1. To form the possessive case (who owns it) of a singular noun (one person or thing), add an apostrophe and an s.

> Example: *the girl's coat   Bill's ball   the car's tire*

2. To form the possessive case of a plural noun (two or more people or things) ending in s, add only the apostrophe.

> Example: *the boys' car   the cars' headlights*

3. Do not use an apostrophe for: *his, hers, its, ours, yours, theirs, whose.*

> Example: T*he car was theirs.   The school must teach its students.*

4. Indefinite pronouns: (could be anyone) *one, everyone, everybody,* require an apostrophe and an *s* to show possession.

Example: *One's* car is important.   That must be *somebody's* bat.

5. An apostrophe shows where letters have been omitted in a contraction (making one word out of two).

   Example: *can't* for cannot   *don't* for do not
            we've for we have   *doesn't* for does not

   Note that the apostrophe goes in the word where the letter or letters have been left out.

6. Use an apostrophe and an s to make the plural of letters, numbers and of words referred to as words.

   Example: There are three *b's* and two *m's* in that sentence.
            It was good back in the *1970's*.
            Do not say so many *"and so's"* when you explain things.

AUDIENCE

Writers don't just write. They write to selected readers in specific forms for purposes. To be effective, writers must decide what form is most appropriate for their intended readers so that they can accomplish their purposes.

Keep in mind that, just as you talk differently to different audiences, you must write differently also. You wouldn't talk to your mother or your minister the same way you'd talk to friends.

As you read your writing, think of who your intended audiences are and try and judge how what you're saying will influence those people.
   Examples:

1. Informal—colloquial (used with friends in friendly letters and notes):

   Man, that was a such a dumb test, I just flunked it.

2. Semiformal (used in themes, tests, and term papers in school and in letters and articles to businesses and newspapers):

   The test was very hard and so I did not do well.

3. Formal (seldom used by students but appropriate for the most formal of written communication on the highest levels of government, business or education):

   The six-week's examination was of sufficient scope to challenge the knowledge of the best of the students in the class. Not being adequately prepared for it, I did not demonstrate my true ability.

AWKWARD WRITING

Awkward writing is rough and clumsy. It can be confusing to the reader and make the meaning unclear. Many times just the changing of the placement of a word or the changing of a word will clear up the awkwardness.

If you read your work out loud or have someone read it to you and then to listen to what they're saying, you can catch the awkwardness. Remember that you have to read loud enough to hear your own voice.

1. *Each of you kids will have to bring each day each of the following things: pen, pencil and paper.*

This should be rewritten to read:

Each day bring pens, pencils and paper.

2. *The bird flew down near the ground, and having done this, began looking for bugs or worms, because it was easier to see them down low than it had been when it was flying high in the sky.*

There are many problems with that sentence. To get rid of its awkwardness, it could be rewritten to read:

The bird, looking for food, swooped low.

Keep in mind that the point of your writing is for them to give your readers information. The simplest way to do this may be the best way.

CLICHÉ

All young writers like to use expressions they've heard or read. It makes them feel that they're writing like adult authors. Many times you'll use expressions that you didn't realize have been used so many times before that they no longer are fresh and exciting for their readers:

round as a dollar	*pretty as a picture*	*tall as a tree*	*snapped back to reality*
stopped in his tracks	*stone cold dead*	*fell flat on his face*	*roared like a lion*
white as a sheet	*graceful as a swan*	*stiff as a board*	*limber as a willow*

Usually the first expressions young writers think of when they write will be clichés. If you think you've heard of an expression before, don't use it, but think of ways to tell your readers what you want them to know using expressions that are new.

COMMAS

I am including commas because they are often seen as such a problem. Young people cannot learn all of the comma rules at once. Some will never learn them all. All writers have some comma placement rules they ignore. One thing that will help you is to read your work out loud and to listen to where your voices drop inside sentences. That is where a comma goes. This will work for about 95% of comma placement. This works because commas are needed and used to make clear the meaning in writing. They indicate a pause or a separation of ideas.

Rules: You should use commas in the following situations:

1. To separate place names—as in an address, dates, or items in a series
2. To set off introductory or concluding expressions
3. To make clear the parts of a compound sentence
4. To set off transitional or non-restrictive words or expressions in a sentence

Examples:

1. *During the day on May 3, 1989, I began to study.*

I had courses in English, math and geography at a little school in Ann Arbor, Michigan.

The parts of the date should be separated by commas, and the courses in this sentence which come in a list should be separated by commas. You have a choice of whether to put a comma before the and just prior to the last item on a list.

2. *After the bad showing on the test, Bill felt he had to study more than he had.*

The introduction—*After the bad showing on the test*—to the central idea of this sentence—*Bill felt he had to study more*—is set off from this central idea by a comma.

3. *Bill went to class to study for the test, and I went to the snack bar to feed the inner beast.*

There are two complete ideas here: 1) *Bill went to study*; and, 2) *I went to eat.* These two ideas can be joined in a compound (two or more things put together) sentence if there is a conjunction (*and, but, though*) between them and they are separated by a comma. Notice where the comma is placed in the example below.

4. *Bob, who didn't really care, made only five points on the test.*

The idea of this fourth sentence is that Bob made only five points on the test. The information given that he didn't care is interesting but not essential to the understanding of the main idea of the sentence. The commas indicate that the words between them are not essential to the meaning of the sentence.

COMMA SPLICE

A comma splice is when the two halves of a compound sentence are joined/separated by a comma.

Example: *Bill had to take the test over again, he felt sorry he would miss the party.*

A comma splice can be avoided by writing this sentence in one of the five following ways:

1. *Bill had to take the test over again and felt sorry he would miss the party.*

2. *Bill had to take the test over again; he felt sorry he would miss the party.*

3. *Bill had to take the test over again, and he felt sorry he would miss the party.*

4. *Bill had to take the test over again: he felt sorry he would miss the party.*

5. *Bill had to take the test over again. He felt sorry he would miss the party.*

Notice that the punctuation of each of the above examples gives the reader a different idea about Bill and how he felt.

DIALOGUE STRUCTURE and PUNCTUATION

Dialogue is conversation between two or more people. When shown in writing, it refers to the speech or thoughts of characters.

Rules: Dialogue can occur either in the body of the writing or on a separate line for each new speaker.

Examples:
1. *John took his test paper from the teacher and said to him, "This looks like we'll get to know each other well." The teacher looked surprised and said with a smile, "I hope so."*

2. *John took his test paper from the teacher and said to him, "This looks like you and I'll get to know each other well."*
   The teacher looked surprised and said with a smile, "I hope so."

3. *John took his test paper from the teacher and thought, "This looks like I'll get to know this old man well this year." The teacher looked surprised—almost as if he had read John's mind—and thought, "I hope so."*

DICTION

Diction is the words chosen—your vocabulary as you use it.

Rules: There are at least four levels of diction:

1. FORMAL: The words of educated people when they are being serious with each other.

  Example: *Our most recent suggestion was the compromise we felt we could make under the present circumstances.*

2. INFORMAL: Polite conversation of people who are relaxed.

  Example: *We have given you the best offer we could.*

3. COLLOQUIAL: Everyday speech by average people.

  Example: *That was the best we could do.*

4. SLANG: Ways of talking that are never used in writing except in dialogue to show characterization.

  Example: *It's up to you, cook or get outa the kitchen.*

FLOWERY WRITING

You'll use flowery writing when you want to impress your readers with how many good words you can use to express ideas. This results in the words used becoming more important than the ideas presented.

Rule: A general rule that should apply is: What you say should be put as simply as possible.

  Example: *The red and fiery sun slowly settled into the distant hills like some great, billowing sailing ship sinking beyond the horizon. It cast its pink and violet flags along the tops of the clouds where they waved briefly before this ship of light slid beneath the waves of darkness and cast us all, there on the beach, into night.*

  This is so flowery that it is hard to read without laughing. It should be rewritten to read:

  We remained on the beach gazing at the darkening sky while the sun set.

FRAGMENT:

This is part of a sentence which lacks a subject or a verb or both.

Check your sentences to make sure they have both subjects and verbs.

Some writers use fragments effectively. You may do this in your creative writing. You should avoid using fragments in expository papers.

Examples: Fragments can be powerful if used correctly:

When Janet reached her door she found it was partly open. A burglar! Someone had been in her house and had left the door open.

MODIFIER (dangling)

This means that there is nothing for the modifier to modify in the sentence.

Examples: *Getting up, my arms felt tired.* (How did the arms get up all by themselves?)

This should read: *When I got up my arms felt tired.*

Coming down the street, my feet wanted to turn into the park. (Again, how did the feet do this?)

This should read: *Coming down the street, I felt as if my feet wanted to turn toward the park.*

Being almost asleep, the accident made me jump. (It is clear the accident could not have been asleep.)

This should read: *I was almost asleep and the accident made me jump.*

PARAGRAPH

A paragraph is a sentence or a group of sentences developing one idea or topic.

Rules: In nonfiction writing, a paragraph consists of a topic sentence which is supported by other sentences giving additional details. A good rule is: A paragraph in this kind of writing should have at least four supportive sentences, making at least five sentences for every paragraph.

Example:

TOPIC SENTENCE: One sentence that introduces the reader to the main idea of the paragraph.

PARAGRAPH DEVELOPMENT: May be made by facts, examples, incidents, comparison, contrast, definition, reasons (in the form of arguments) or by a combination of methods.

PARALLELISM

Parallelism is two or more parts of a single sentence, having equal importance—being structured the same way.

Examples:

1. *We went home to eat and reading.* This should read: *We went home to eat and to read.* This is obvious in such a short sentence, but this is an easy mistake to make when the sentences get complicated.

2. *There are a number of things that a boy must think about when he is planning to take a bike trip. He must think about checking the air pressure in his tires, putting oil on the chain, making sure the batteries in his light are fresh and to make sure his brakes work properly.*

Notice that in this list there is a combination of four parallel participles and one infinitive which cannot be parallel in structure. (This sounds like English-teacher talk.)

What it means is the first three items on the list: (1) *checking,* (2) *putting* (3) *making* are parallel, but the fourth item on the list, (4) *to make,* is not structured the same way, and so this last item is not parallel in structure with the first three items.

This sentence should be rewritten to read: *He must think about checking the air pressure in his tires, putting oil on the chain, making sure the batteries in his light are fresh and making sure his brakes work properly.*

PRONOUN REFERENCE and AGREEMENT

To keep writing from being boring, pronouns are often used instead of nouns.

Rules: It must be clear to the reader which noun the pronoun is replacing. The pronoun must agree in case, gender and number with that noun. The most common error young writers make is with number agreement.

Examples:

Betty and Janet went to the show, but she didn't think it was so good. (It's not clear which girl didn't like the show.)

If a child comes to dinner without clean hands, they must go back to the sink and wash over. (The word *they* refers to "a child" and the number is mixed. This should read: If children come to dinner without clean hands they should go back. . .)

Both boys took exams but Bob got a higher score on it. (The pronoun *it* refers to the noun exams and the number is mixed here.)

Everybody should go to the show, and they should have their tickets handy. (The problem here is that the word everybody is singular and the pronouns they and their are plural.) The following words are singular and they need singular verbs: *everybody, anybody, each, someone.* This could read: *Everybody should go to the show, and each girl should have her ticket handy.*

QUOTATION MARKS

Quotation marks are used to indicate exact words or thoughts and to indicate short works and chapters of long works.

Rule 1.   You should put in quotation marks the direct quotation of a person's words. When you use other marks of punctuation with quotation marks: 1) you should put commas and periods inside the quotation marks; and, 2) put other punctuation marks inside the quotation marks if they are part of the quotation; if they are not part of the quotation, you should put them outside of the quotation marks.

Example: *The salesman said, "This is the gum all the kids are chewing."*

Rule 2.   Put in quotation marks the titles of chapters, articles, other parts of books or magazines, short poems, short stories and songs.

Example: *In this magazine there were two things I really liked: "The Wind Blows Free" and "Flowers," the poems by the young girl.*

REDUNDANCY

Redundancy means using different words to say the same thing. The writer doesn't gain by this, only confuses and bores the reader.

Examples: *I, myself, feel it is true.*
It is *plain* and *clear* to see.
Today, in the world, there *is* not room for lack of care for the ecology.

This is an easy mistake to make, and it will take conscious thought for you to avoid this problem. You'll have to have help to find redundancies in your work. There are no exercises you can do which will help; just use care when you're proofreading your work.

RUN-ON SENTENCE:

This is the combining of two or more sentences as if they were one.

> Example: *Bill saw that the fish was too small he put it back in the lake and then put a fresh worm on his hook.* (This sentence needs to be broken into two sentences by putting a period between small and he. It could also be correct with a semicolon between small and he.)

SENTENCE VARIETY

Young writers have a tendency to structure all or most of their sentences in the same way.

Give variety to the structuring of your sentences. A common problem for young writers is that of beginning most sentences with a subject-verb pattern.

> Examples: *<u>Janet bought</u> a car. The <u>car was</u> blue. <u>It had</u> a good radio. <u>She liked</u> her car and spent a lot of time in it.*

These sentences could be re-written and combined so they all do not start with a subject and verb.

> *The car Janet bought was blue. Because she liked it so much, she spent a lot of time in it.*

SUBJECT-VERB AGREEMENT (number)

Closely related words have matching forms, and, when the forms match, they agree. Subjects and their verbs agree if they both are singular or both are plural.

Rules: Singular subjects require singular verbs, and plural subjects require plural verbs.

Singular: *car, man, that, she, he, it*

Plural: *cars, men, those, women, they*

Singular: *The heater was good.   The heater works well.*

Plural: *The heaters were good.   The heaters work well.*

Most nouns form their plural by adding the letter *s*, as in *bats* and *cats*. The clue is the final *s*.

It is just the opposite with most verbs. A verb ending in *s* is usually singular, as in *puts, yells, is* and *was*.

Most verbs not ending in *s* are plural, as in *they put, they yell*. The exceptions are verbs used with *I* and singular *you*: *I put, you put.*

Problems come when there is a phrase or clause between the subject and verb.

Example: *This red car, which is just one of a whole lot full of cars, is owned by John and Bob.* (It is easy for some young writers to think that cars is the plural subject and incorrectly write the sentence this way: *This red car, which is just one of a whole lot full of cars, are owned by John and Bob.* The subject of this sentence *This red car* is singular; there are just a lot of words between the subject and the verb, and it confuses the number.)

TENSE ERROR

Tense errors occur when past and present tenses are mixed and there is no justification for changing.

Rules:

1. Present tense is used to describe actions that are taking place at the time of the telling of the event.

   Example: *John is in the house. Mr. Jones lives there.*

2. Past tense is used to describe actions that have already happened.

   Example: *John was in the house. Mr. Jones lived there.*

3. Future tense is used to describe actions that will happen.

   Example: *John will be in the house. Mr. Jones will live there.*

TRANSITIONS

Transitions are bridges from one idea to the next or from one reference to the next or from one section of a paper to the next.

Rule: It will help your readers if you aid them in their reading by bridging their ideas for them. This can be done by:

1. Using linking words like: however, moreover, thus, and because and phrases like: on the other hand, in effect, and as an example.

2. Repeating words and phrases used earlier in the writing.

3. Referring to points used previously.

Examples: If you were to write two paragraphs about pets—a cat and a dog, it would be necessary for you to make some transition between the two paragraphs—the one about the cat and the one about the dog.

Below is the ending of a paragraph about a cat and the beginning of a paragraph about a dog. The idea of having fun with the cat will serve as a transition to the paragraph about having fun with the dog.

   . . .and so I get a great deal of pleasure from my cat. She and I have a lot of fun together.
   My dog, on the other hand, gives me pleasure and fun of a different nature. We spend time. . .

VOICE   (passive and active)

Most sentences are built on the order of subject-verb-object. This produces an active voice. If a passive verb is used, it inverts this order and makes it seem as if the object were doing rather than receiving the action of the verb.

Your writing will be more forceful if you use an active voice.

Examples:

Active: *Bill threw the ball.   We must spend this money.   Bill drove the car with care.*

Passive: *The ball was thrown by Bill.   This money must be spent by us.*
The car was driven with care by Bill.

Rule: You can use a passive voice if:

1. The doer of the action is unknown

2. The action needs to be emphasized

3. The receiver of the action is of more importance than the doer of the action.

Examples:
1. *When we were gone, the house was burglarized.*   (The one who broke in is unknown.)

2. *No matter how hard they played, the game was lost.* (The game being lost is the most important thing.)

3. *My pet mouse was eaten by that cat.* (The mouse is more important than the cat.)

WRONG WORD

The words you use do not always mean what you think they do.

Rule:
You should not try and use words in your writing that you don't feel comfortable with while talking.
If you would never say the words *alas* or *to no avai*l or *travail*, you should not write them.

ISBN 1-888344-09-1

Order Form

To place your *Writing Strands* order, simply fill out this form and send it to us by mail or by fax. If you would like to get your order started even faster, go to the *Writing Strands* website and place your order online at: www.writingstrands.com

			QTY	Total
Writing Strands 1 Oral Work for ages 3-8		$15 ea.	___	_____
Writing Strands 2 About 7 years old		$20 ea.	___	_____
Writing Strands 3 Starting program ages 8-12		$20 ea.	___	_____
Writing Strands 4 Any age after Level 3 or starting program at age 13 or 14		$20 ea.	___	_____
Writing Strands 5 Any age after Level 4 or starting program at age 15 or 16		$20 ea.	___	_____
Writing Strands 6 17 or any age after Level 5		$20 ea.	___	_____
Writing Strands 7 18 or any age after Level 6		$20 ea.	___	_____
Writing Exposition Senior high school and after Level 7		$20 ea.	___	_____
Creating Fiction Senior high school and after Level 7		$20 ea.	___	_____
Evaluating Writing Parents′ manual for all levels of *Writing Strands*		$20 ea.	___	_____
Reading Strands Parents′ manual for story and book interpretation, all grades		$20 ea.	___	_____
Communication and Interpersonal Relationships Communication Manners (teens)		$20 ea.		

Basic Starter Set (SAVE $5.00)
Writing Strands 2, Writing Strands 3, Reading Strands and *Evaluating Writing* — $75 per set ___ _____

Intermediate Starter Set (SAVE $10.00)
Writing Strands 3, Writing Strands 4, Evaluating Writing, Communication and Interpersonal Relationships and *Reading Strands* — $90 per set ___ _____

Advanced Starter Set (SAVE $30.00)
Writing Strands 5, Writing Strands 6, Writing Strands 7, Writing Exposition, Creating Fiction, Evaluating Writing, Communication and Interpersonal Relationships and *Reading Strands* — $130 per set ___ _____

Dragonslaying Is for Dreamers Ð Package
1st novel in *Dragonslaying* trilogy (Early teens) and parents′ manual for analyzing the novel. — $18.95 ea. ___ _____

Dragonslaying Is for Dreamers
Novel only — $9.95 ea. ___ _____

Axel Meets the Blue Men
2nd novel in *Dragonslaying* trilogy (Teens) — $9.95 ea. ___ _____

Axel′ Challenge
Final novel in *Dragonslaying* trilogy (Teens) — $9.95 ea. ___ _____

Dragonslaying Trilogy
All three novels in series — $25 set ___ _____

Dragonslaying Trilogy and Parents′ Manual
Three novels plus parents′ manual for first novel — $32.99 set ___ _____

SUBTOTAL (use this total to calculate shipping) _____

Texas residents: Add 8.25% sales tax _____

All Orders Shipping: Add $6 for orders $75 and under _____

Add $8 for orders over $75 _____

Canada Shipping: Add $6

Outside US/Canada Shipping: Add $14 _____

TOTAL U.S. FUNDS _____

Mail your check or money order or fill in your credit card information below:

☐ VISA   ☐ Discover   ☐ Master Card

Account Number_____

Expiration date: Month _____ Year _____

Signature **X** _____

We ship UPS to the 48 states, so please no P.O. Box addresses. PLEASE PRINT

Name _____

Street _____

City _____ State ____ Zip _____

Phone (_____) _____

Email _____

SHIPPING INFORMATION
CONTINENTAL U.S.: We ship via UPS ground service. Most customers will receive their orders within 10 business days.

ALASKA, HAWAII, U.S. MILITARY ADDRESSES AND US TERRITORIES: We ship via U.S. Priority Mail. Orders generally arrive within 2 weeks.

OUTSIDE U.S.: We generally ship via Air Mail. Delivery times vary.

RETURNS
Our books are guaranteed to please you. If they do not, return them within 30 days and we′ll refund the full purchase price.

PRIVACY
We respect your privacy. We will not sell, rent or trade your personal information.

INQUIRIES AND ORDERS
Phone: (800) 688-5375
Fax: (888) 663 7855 TOLL FREE
Write: *Writing Strands*
624 W. University, Suite 248T
Denton, TX 76201-1889
E-mail: info@writingstrands.com
Website: www.writingstrands.com

TO ORDER EVEN FASTER, GO ONLINE AT:
www.writingstrands.com

Prices valid through 3/31/08